Family "Playbook"

A Collection of Recipes, Family Photos, Personal Quotes, Statistics & Trivia!

Benefitting the Children at Happy Hill Farm Academy/Home

Dallas Cowboys Wives

The Dallas Cowboys Family "Playbook"

A Collection of Recipes, Family Photos, Personal Quotes, Statistics & Trivia!

Published by TPG, Inc.
Dallas, Texas
First Printing: September 1997

Happy Hill Farm Academy/Home
HC 51, Box 56
Granbury, Texas 76048

Acknowledgments

To every player, coach, and Cowboys administration—plus their wives and families—who had a part in making this year's "Dallas Cowboys Family Playbook" a reality, we give our special thanks.

Our gratitude to Brooke and Dale Hellestrae, and Tasha and Tony Tolbert, who worked very hard at gathering the materials for this volume. Thanks, also, to all of the wives—players, coaches, and administration—for your cooperation in providing the materials to be used for the "Family Playbook." We would be remiss if we did not include Charlyn Aikman and Carol Hitt in that special group as well.

We're especially grateful for the encouragement and cooperation of these friends in the administrative office without whose assistance this "Family Playbook, 1997" would not be: Charlotte (Jones) Anderson, Doreen Bice, Marylyn Love, Laura Fryar, and Bridgette Smith.

A thank you, also, to the public relations office—including Rich Dalrymple, Emily Cruz, Brett Daniels, and Doug Hood—who are always kind to provide pictures, when needed.

A special tribute to Jim Maurer, the Dallas Cowboys Head Trainer, and his wife, Rosanne. Jim is the Farm's link to the Ed Block Courage Award Foundation.

Thanks to the TV production department—John Chang, Brandi Drawe, Roger Greene, and Scott Purcel—for their assistance in providing film for marketing.

Design concept and art for the book cover were provided by Access Creative and Web Life Productions in Fort Worth, Texas—with photography by Smiley's Studio, also in Fort Worth. Lisa Ober-Schleicher (St. Louis, Missouri) drew the illustrations used throughout the "Family Playbook", and James Smith provided fill-in photos. Thank you, Lisa and James.

Our further appreciation to Russ Russell, Jim Browder, and all of the wonderful Dallas Cowboys "Weekly" staff, for their help with production photos.

And to the two real "brains" behind the new "Family Playbook" concept, and the folks who did most of the work: Gloria, my wife; and Stacy Gilbert, my associate.

Our thanks to Jay Heinlein, and John Ward of Trophy Publishing; and Barry and Virginia Kerrigan and Del LeMond of Desktop Miracles, Inc. in Dallas, Texas—for designing and producing the interior, and for handling printing and production details.

What you all have done in the creation of the all-new "Playbook" is to provide Happy Hill Farm Academy/Home with a vehicle for raising money for the Farm's Scholarship Fund for indigent children. God bless each of you as we together reach out a helping hand to the hurting children around us. The "Family Playbook" is a means to this end.

C. Edward Shipman
Executive Director
Happy Hill Farm Academy/Home

The Dallas Cowboys Courage House

at Happy Hill Farm Academy/Home

THE DALLAS COWBOYS
COURAGE HOUSE
AT HAPPY HILL FARM ACADEMY/HOME
"Where, since 1975, deserving boys and girls live, work, and study, free from abuse and neglect."

Two years ago, Jerry Jones and a group of Cowboys players came to the campus of Happy Hill Farm Academy/ Home to dedicate the Dallas Cowboys Courage house officially. The Dallas Cowboys Courage House is the sixth such home for abused children. Other Courage Houses are located in the following NFL cities: Detroit, Chicago, Pittsburgh, Miami, and Baltimore. The long-range goal of the Ed Block Courage Award Foundation is to establish a Courage House in every NFL city. The seventh will open this year in New York.

The partnership embodied with the Courage House logo represents the commitment of the NFL, NFL Charities, NFL Alumni, Players Association, PFATS, and the Ed Block Courage Award Foundation. The commitment is to provide shelter, treatment, and prevention programs to victims of child abuse and domestic violence.

Courage House

NATIONAL SUPPORT NETWORK

Each year, since 1984, the Ed Block Courage Award Foundation honors those NFL players who exemplify courage in the face of overwhelming odds. The award is usually presented to a player, voted by his peers, who has come back from some career-threatening injury to play once again.

Dallas Cowboys Recipients of the Ed Block Courage Award are as follows: 1984 - James Jones; 1985 - Howard Richards;

1986 - Anthony Dorsett; 1987 - Brian D. Baldinger; 1988 - Randy White; 1989 - Ed "Too Tall" Jones; 1990 - Kelvin Martin; 1991 - Ken Norton, Jr.; 1992 - Daryl Johnston; 1993 - Bill Bates; 1994 - Mark Stepnoski; 1995 - Erik Williams; and this year's (1996) winner is Kevin Smith.

Happy Hill Farm Academy/Home is pleased to be a part of this growing national organization dedicated to reaching out a helping hand to abused and neglected children.

Happy Hill Farm Academy/Home

"Where Tomorrow Begins"

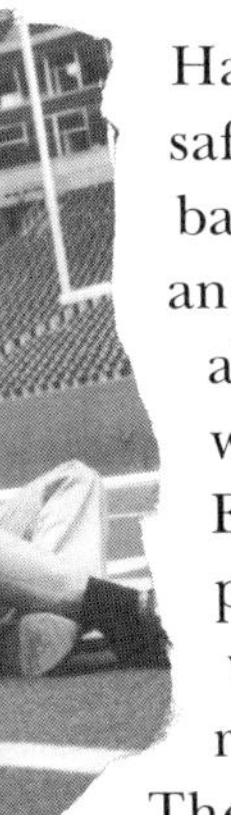

Happy Hill Farm Academy/Home is a safe haven for children who come from backgrounds of neglect and abuse. Helen and Riley (the two children on the cover), along with 100 other boys and girls, live, work, and study at Happy Hill Farm. Every child at Happy Hill Farm is in desperate need of help if they are to survive and become independent, responsible, productive young adults. The purchase of this Cookbook is literally giving these children another chance in life.

Happy Hill Farm Academy/Home is a 500-acre working farm, located southwest of Fort Worth between Granbury and Glen Rose, Texas.

Uniqueness of the Program . . .

The Farm is different from many other child-care facilities, because Happy Hill Farm does not receive any State or Federal funds, nor United Way monies. The program is solely funded by the private sector . . . corporations, foundations, and individuals just like you!

Happy Hill Farm Children's Home is licensed by the Texas Department of

Protective and Regulatory Services. Happy Hill Farm Academy is accredited by the Southern Association of Colleges and Schools and is a member of the Texas Association of Private and Parochial Schools and the Texas Association of Non-Public Schools.

Additionally, Happy Hill Farm has a fully-accredited (K-12 grades) private school on campus. Classes are very small, and teachers are trained to work with emotionally-disturbed children. Each child receives the help necessary to succeed in school.

Who Comes to Happy Hill Farm . . .

Boys and girls, 5 to 18 years of age, are considered for admission without regard to race, religion, or ethnic origin. There are boys and girls from any number of racial backgrounds on campus.

The Farm and the Program . . .

The 500-acre rolling farm/campus contains thirteen homestyle living units. Each is home to eight boys or girls. There is a husband-wife houseparent couple in each living unit. There are athletic fields, a gym, barns, dining center, vocational greenhouse, agricultural buildings, and a woodshop.

The accredited private school focuses on high academic standards, but it also allows the students to participate in supplementary programs, such as art and music—each designed to impart knowledge, sharpen skills, and build self-esteem.

As a working farm, Happy Hill Farm raises its own beef, pork, and lamb. There are horses and a host of pets for the children. The 4-H program is very active. The students care for their livestock projects daily, and blue ribbons adorn the wall of the classroom. A large garden provides foodstuffs for the dining center. Additionally, the land is used to grow grain and hay crops for the livestock.

Happy Hill Farm's boys' and girls' teams excel in track, football, volleyball, basketball, and baseball while competing in the Texas Association of Private and Parochial Schools. The gym's trophy case is jammed, bearing testimony to the students' hard work and athletic abilities.

Moral and Spiritual Aspect . . .

Although the Farm is Christian and has strong moral and spiritual underpinnings, it is not connected to any church or denominational group. The highest moral, ethical, and spiritual values are taught. Children from any or no religious background are offered care.

Twenty-two Years of Blood, Sweat, and Tears . . .

It was 1974—Ed and Gloria Shipman, in their forties, lived in their country home on acreage just outside of Dallas-Fort Worth. Ed was happy in his ministry and work. Their two sons, Chuck and Todd, were sixteen and fourteen years of age. The family was "comfortable." Little did they realize that a telephone call for help from a local marshall was about to change the whole course of their lives. In response to that marshall's appeal for help, the Shipmans took briefly into their home two teenage runaway sisters. In an effort to find a permanent home for the girls, the Shipmans visited child-care facilities throughout Texas. The sisters were finally placed in a small children's home in Texas . . . but the Shipman family had been gripped emotionally. They were now primarily aware of the desperate plight of thousands of America's hurting boys and girls—the"drop-outs" and "kicked-outs" of society.

A year later . . . 1975, with personal financial resources sufficient to last only a few years—but with, what they felt, to be a sense of Divine direction—the Shipmans opened their hearts, and officially opened the doors of Happy Hill Farm Academy/Home, to a group of young boys.

The Cowboy Connection . . .

In 1996, the Dallas Cowboys Courage House was dedicated on the campus of Happy Hill Farm. The Courage House is part of the Ed Block Courage Award Foundation, a national support network dedicated to helping abused children.

Funding . . .

Most of the children who come to the Farm have little or no money for their care. Scholarships—underwritten by individuals, clubs, corporations, and special projects—like the "Dallas Cowboys Wives' Cookbooks"—help to pay for clothing, school books, food, and all the many things that it takes to raise healthy, happy children.

Happy Hill Farm Academy/Home is a non-profit, charitable, Texas corporation and is operated almost entirely with contributions from the private sector. Fees and tuitions from student families account for only a small portion (less than

8%) of the Farm's annual operating budget. All gifts of money, stocks, bonds, property, or gifts-in-kind are tax-deductible.

Here's How Your Gifts Are Used

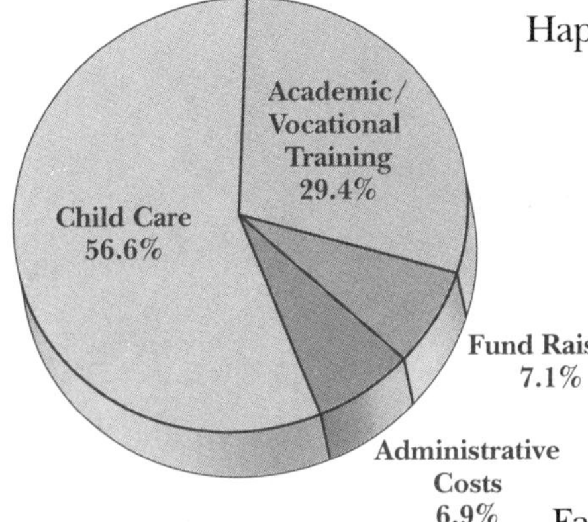

Happy Hill Farm Academy/ Home's Founder and Executive Director and the Farm's Board of Directors believe strongly in financial accountability. The Farm utilizes the services of a recognized certified public accountant and one of the Metroplex's largest law firms. Happy Hill Farm has an annual audit. The Farm has worked tirelessly to keep these promotional costs and administrative costs to the bare minimum. Since Happy Hill Farm Academy/ Home receives no State or Federal funds, nor any United Way monies, the Farm is totally dependent on the gifts from its friends in the private sector. The monies you send to Happy Hill Farm go directly to care for the children. If you wish to help financially, volunteer your time or services, or get involved in some other way, please write or call:

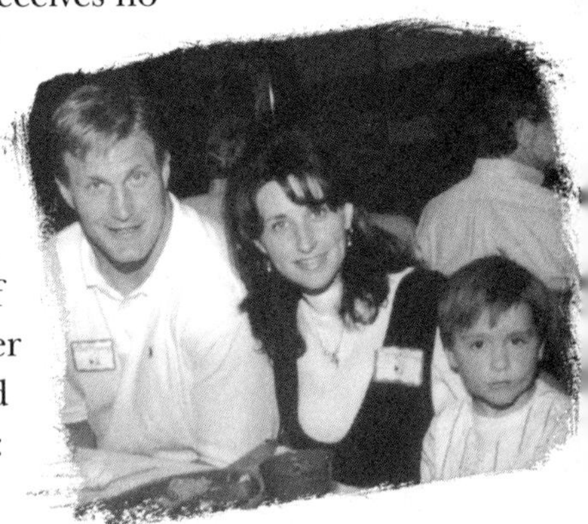

Happy Hill Farm
HC 51, Box 56
Granbury, Texas 76048
Phone: (254) 897-4822

1997 Dallas Cowboys and Their Wives

Table of Contents

Acknowledgments iii
Dallas Cowboys Courage House v
Happy Hill Farm Academy/Home vii

Administration

Jerry & Gene Jones 3
Pear and Hazelnut Tarts • Cascadilla Soup
Stephen & Karen Jones 7
Rice and Artichoke Casserole
Charlotte & Shy Anderson 11
Lasagna • Lemon Pound Cake - with a Twist
Jerry Jones, Jr. 15
Southwestern Omelet
Barry Switzer 17
Italian Eggs • Pasta Fagioli

Players

Troy Aikman 23
Beef Supper • Vegetable-Rice Casserole • Troy's Favorite Chocolate Chip Cookies
Larry & Janelle Allen 27
Tamale Pie • Old-Fashioned Potato Soup • Gingerbread
Antonio Anderson 31
Special Hamburgers • Beefy Baked Beans
Bill & Denise Bates 35
Breakfast Burritos • Chicken and Dumplings • Chicken Salad
Darren & Teresa Benson 41
Rotel Chicken • Eggnog Pie
Eric Bjornson 45
Bow-Tie Pasta
Macey Brooks 49
Spanish Rice • Almond Danish
Shante Carver 53
Cauliflower Bake
Tony & Tamara Casillas 57
Limeade Grilled Chicken • Spring Primavera
Dexter Coakley 61
Special Cookies • Chicken with Cucumbers in Paprika Sauce
Richie & Kristin Cunningham 65
Mr. C's Seafood Gumbo

Billy Davis 69
Potato/Cheddar Cheese Soup • Honey Crunch Cookies
Wendell Davis 73
Chili • Lemonade
John & Kristine Flannery 77
Quiche • Cream Cheese Tarts
Scott Galbraith 81
Oven-Roasted Potatoes • Orange Carrots
Jason & Brill Garrett 83
Jason and Brill's Baked French Toast
Randall Godfrey 87
Devil's Food Cake
Toby Gowin 91
Baked Stuffed Flounder • Superior Squash Casserole
Darryl Hardy 95
Fantastic Burgers • Crab Meat Dip • Grits Supreme Casserole
George Hegamin 99
Marinated/Grilled Lamb Chops • Choice Apple Cake
Dale & Brooke Hellestrae 101
Shrimp Spring Rolls • Double-Chocolate Waffles
Chad & Tammy Hennings 107
Wisconsin Cheese Soup • Honey-Lemon Chicken
Michael & Sandy Irvin 111
Black-Eyed Peas and Shrimp Salad • Herb-Baked Catfish
Daryl & Diane Johnston 115
Cornbread Sausage Stuffing with Apples
David & Melody LaFleur 119
Crawfish Fettucini • Pralines
Leon Lett 123
Incomparable Bread Pudding
Brock & Keri Marion 125
Chocolate No-Bake Cookies • Chocolate Banana Bread
Kevin Mathis 129
Ham and Potatoes au Gratin • Mexican-Style Pork Ribs
Hurvin McCormack 131
Unique Deviled Eggs • Apple Cider Pound Cake
Anthony Miller 135
All-American Creamy Coleslaw • Chicken and Dumplings in Herbed Broth
Singor Mobley 139
Singor's Dishwasher Salmon • Banana Bread
Nate & Dorothy Newton 143
Barbecued Spareribs • Old-Fashioned Peach Cobbler
Kavika Pittman 147
Rhubarb Pie
Deion Sanders 151
Salmon Croquettes • Chicken Fajita Salad

Steve Scifres 155
Chicken Marsala • Caesar Salad
Clay Shiver 159
Shrimp Dip • Spinach Casserole
Emmitt Smith 163
Amaretto Cheesecake
Kevin Smith 167
Shrimp Etouffee • Savory Crab Cakes
Vinson & Anne Smith 171
Star Cheese Bites • Chicken and Asparagus Casserole
Omar Stoutmire 175
Chocolate-Blueberry Squares
Fred & Shay Strickland 177
Apple Cherry Cobbler • Orange Muffins
Nicky Sualua 181
Jalapeno Cornbread Muffins
Broderick Thomas 183
Fresh Corn Pudding
Tony & Tasha Tolbert 187
Conna's Corn Dip • Flounder Grilled in Foil
Mark & Pono Tuinei 191
Miracle Bars • Impossible Taco Pie
Herschel & Cindy Walker 197
Minestrone Soup
Kenny Wheaton 201
Pumpkin Pie in Spiced Nut Crust
Charlie Williams 205
French Dip Sandwiches • Awesome Brownies
Erik Williams 207
Baked Beans Western-Style • Barbecued Pork Chops
Sherman Williams 211
Crab Bake Sandwich • French Chocolate
Stepfret Williams 213
Crawfish Fettucine • Coconut Pie
Wade & Kathy Wilson 217
Chicken Pot Pie • Chocolate Layered Dessert
Darren & Juli Woodson 221
Lemon Poppy Seed Cake • Spicy Catfish

Coaches & Staff

Hubbard & Gloria Alexander 227
Buttermilk Baked Chicken
Joe & Diann Avezzano 231
Olive Oil and Balsamic Bread Dip
Jim & Beverly Bates 233
Gazpacho

Charlie & Stephanie Biggurs 235
Zesty Meatloaf

Robert & Diana Blackwell 239
Crab Cakes Maryland • Joe's Florida Stone Crab Mustard Sauce

Craig Boller 241
Mexican Lasagna

Joe & Joyce Brodsky 245
Jeff Brodsky's Hot (No-Fry) Crispy Wings

Britt & Laura Brown 247
Pasta and Sausage Dish • Britt's Mom's Chicken Spaghetti

Bucky & Amy Buchanan 251
Santa Fe Chicken • Pineapple Cake

Dave & Kay Campo 253
Baby Back Ribs

Rich & Ros Dalrymple 257
Chicken Marinade • Rustic Potato Wedges

Robert & Janice Ford 259
Our Friend Fran's Flank Steak Marinade • Corn Pudding

Bob & Emily Haas 263
Chicken Teriyaki • Fruit Salad with Honey-Lime Dressing

Tommy & Cherrie Hart 265
Toffee Cake

Steve & Raffy Hoffman 267
Cheese Potatoes • Garlic and Rosemary Pork Roast

Hudson & Elsie Houck 269
Capitol Chicken • Artichoke Dip

Joe & Camille Juruszek 273
Pasta and Broccoli • Twice-Baked Potatoes

Jim & Rosanne Maurer 275
Marinated Pasta Salad • Low-Fat Quesadillas

Bruce & Kathy Mays 279
Bruce's Shrimp 'n Rice • Kathy's Philly Fruit Pizza

Mike & Jan McCord 281
Chocolate Cake

Clancy Pendergast 285
Scalloped Potatoes • German Apple Cake

Bill & D'Ann Priakos 287
Crawfish Etouffee

Jack & Wendy Reilly 291
Lewis & Clark's White Chili • Easy Dessert Fondue

Ernie & Joyce Zampese 293
Judy Epplers' Hawaiian Tart

Mike & Vikki Zimmer 297
Vikki's One-Pan Potatoes and Chicken Dijon • Zimmer Kids' Jell-O Popcorn

Recipe Index 300

Administration

Jerral "Jerry" & Gene Jones

Dallas Cowboys
Front Office
Owner/President &
General Manager

What I Value Most

"Family." — *Jerry and Gene*

Jerry and Gene Jones - at San Francisco, 1996

If I Were Not in Professional Football I Would Be

"Sailing the Mediterranean." — *Gene*

BORN

Jerry - 10-13-42

Gene - 2-14-42

COLLEGE

Jerry - Arkansas

Gene - Arkansas

CHILDREN

Stephen - 33 years

Charlotte Jones Anderson - 31 years

Jerry, Jr. - 28 years

GRANDCHILDREN

Jessica Jones - 5 years

Jordan Jones - 4 years

Caroline Jones - newborn

Haley Anderson - 4 years

Shy Anderson, Jr. - 2 years

YEARS IN NFL

9th year

Purchased Dallas Cowboys

February 25, 1989

The Jones Family - Charlotte Anderson, Jerry, Gene, Stephen, and Jerry, Jr.

Favorite Holiday or Holiday Tradition

"Christmas morning - breakfast with the entire family." —*Jerry and Gene*

Hobbies and Other Interests

"Tennis, spending time with our grandchildren, and snow skiing." —*Jerry*

"Walking on the beach, spending time with our grandchildren, and snow skiing." — *Gene*

Jerry and Gene Jones with their grandchildren - left to right: Jerry (holding Haley and Shy Anderson, Jr.); Gene, with Jessica and Jordan Jones

Pear and Hazelnut Tarts

(Favorite from Chef Leslie Gething)

TART PASTRY

- 1¼ cups flour
- ½ cup unsalted butter, slightly softened
- 1 egg
- pinch of salt
- ½ cup water (or, as needed)

FILLING

- 3 Bartlett, Anjou, or other pears, poached in red wine syrup
- 6 tablespoons ground hazelnuts
- 6 tablespoons sugar

Mix pastry ingredients. Roll out dough, and fit into six, removable bottom, tart shell pans; trim shells, and chill. Cut poached pears into halves; slice halves into even pieces. Mix sugar and hazelnuts, and sprinkle evenly into the tart shells; top nuts with pears. Sprinkle pears with a bit more sugar; bake tarts at 400 degrees (approximately 15 to 20 minutes), until crust is cooked. While tarts are baking, reduce pear poaching liquid, until it is slightly-thickened. Brush this glaze over the tarts when they come from the oven.

Cascadilla Soup

(Favorite from Chef Leslie Gething)

- 4 cups tomato juice
- 1 cup yogurt, or sour cream
- 1 green pepper, finely-diced
- 1 peeled and seeded cucumber, finely-diced
- 2 tablespoons honey (or, to taste)
- 1 clove crushed garlic (optional)
- 2 scallions, finely-minced
- 1 tablespoon chopped dill
- dash of Tabasco sauce
- salt, to taste

Mix all ingredients; chill well. Is best if eaten within 24 hours.

Karen - with daughters: Jessica, Jordan, & Caroline
in Destin, Florida (July, 1997)

Three People I Would Invite to a "Fantasy" Dinner Party

"Vince Lombardi, John F. Kennedy, and Winston Churchill." — *Stephen*

Former Cowboys Player/Coach Most Admired and Why

"Roger Staubach." — *Stephen*

"Bob Lilly." — *Karen*

Game Day Rituals

"Wear lucky clothes, and arrive four hours early at the stadium." — *Stephen*

My Last Meal Would Be

"Steak or pasta." — *Stephen*

"Pasta." — *Karen*

Favorite Childhood Snack

"Rice Crispy treats." — *Stephen*

"Homemade ice cream with strawberry short cake." — *Karen*

Stephen & Karen Jones

Dallas Cowboys
Front Office
Vice President /
Director of
Player Personnel

What I Value Most

"My family." — *Stephen*
"My husband and children." — *Karen*

Stephen Jones with new daughter, Caroline - 3 months (July, 1997)

BORN

Stephen - 6-21-64

Karen - 8-9-64

COLLEGE

Stephen - Arkansas

Karen - Arkansas

CHILDREN

Jessica - 4 years

Jordan - 3 years

Caroline - newborn

PETS

Maggie and Sadie - Golden Retrievers

YEARS IN NFL

8 years

Dallas Cowboys

Biggest Challenge Ever Faced in Life

"The loss of loved ones." — *Stephen and Karen*

If I Were Not in Professional Football I Would Be

"In the real estate business." — *Stephen*

Favorite Holiday or Holiday Tradition

"Christmas." — *Stephen and Karen*

Favorite City outside of Dallas

"Stuttgart, Arkansas." — *Stephen*

"San Francisco, California." — *Karen*

Hobbies and Other Interests

"Hunting, fishing, skiing, and tennis." — *Stephen*

Most Memorable Moment in Life outside of Pro-Football

"Birth of our three daughters." — *Stephen and Karen*

Favorite Time of Day and Why

"After dinner - time spent with kids." — *Stephen*

"Early morning, before anyone else is awake - having a cup of coffee and reading the paper." — *Karen*

Jones girls: Jordan (3 years); and Jessica (4 years)

Rice & Artichoke Casserole

- ¾ cup butter
- 7 green onions and tops, chopped
- 2 cans (4-ounce) sliced mushrooms, drained
- 4 teaspoons dry mustard
- 1 can (16-ounce) artichoke hearts, coarsely-chopped
- 2½ cups cooked rice
- dash of Tabasco sauce
- salt and pepper, to taste
- ½ cup dry sauterne

Sauté onions in butter; add other ingredients. Place in 1½-quart casserole. Bake at 350 degrees for 20 minutes.

Jessica, Stephen, and Jordan - trout fishing on White River in Arkansas

Three People I Would Invite to a "Fantasy" Dinner Party

"The Pope, Robert Redford, and Barbra Streisand." — *Charlotte*

My Last Meal Would Be

"Fried zucchini, fried Mozzarella, and fresh pasta." — *Charlotte*

"Meatloaf and mashed potatoes." — *Shy*

Charlotte Anderson, with son - Shy, Jr.

Favorite Holiday or Holiday Tradition

"Christmas Eve - large family dinner and midnight church service bring out the true meaning of Christmas." — *Charlotte*

Shy, with children - Shy, Jr. and Haley

Favorite City outside of Dallas

"Florence, Italy." — *Charlotte*

Hobbies and Other Interests

"Dancing, skiing, reading, and relaxing!" — *Charlotte*

"Golf, tennis, and working out." — *Shy*

Most Memorable Moment in Life outside of Pro-Football

"The day our children were born." — *Charlotte and Shy*

Favorite Time of Day and Why

"First thing in the morning, right as the children are waking up - they look like sweet angels!" — *Charlotte*

Charlotte Jones & D. Shy Anderson

Dallas Cowboys
Front Office
Vice President /
Director of
Marketing &
Special Events

Philosophy to Live by

"Have faith in yourself and God, and others will have faith in you." — *Charlotte*

The Anderson Family at Texas Stadium

Best Advice I Could Give to a High School Senior

"Enjoy life to its fullest, while keeping your #1 focus on education." — *Charlotte*

What I Value Most

"My family." — *Charlotte and Shy*

Best Asset

"My children and family." — *Charlotte*

"My family." — *Shy*

Favorite Childhood Snack

"Gingerbread and brownies — still are!" — *Charlotte*

"Nutter Butters and Fig Newtons." — *Shy*

BORN

Charlotte - 7-26-66

Shy - 4-3-64

COLLEGE

Charlotte - Stanford

Shy - Arkansas

SPOUSE'S OCCUPATION

Sr. Vice President - Alltel Communications

ANNIVERSARY

June 8 - 6 years

CHILDREN

Haley - 4 years

Shy, Jr. - 2 years

PETS

Star - Chocolate Lab

Lasagna

1 box lasagna pasta
1 carton (16-ounce) small curd cottage cheese
2 eggs
1 package (10-ounce) chopped frozen spinach, thawed and well-drained
1 pound Mozzarella cheese
1 large jar prepared spaghetti sauce (meatless)
2 pounds ground beef
1 pound ground pork
1 large onion, finely-chopped
4 garlic cloves, finely-chopped
1 tablespoon oregano
salt and pepper, to taste
1 large can tomatoes, chopped and undrained
1 cup grated Parmesan cheese

Cook pasta, drain, and rinse in cold water; set aside. Add 1 tablespoon oil to cooking water (to prevent pasta sticking); drain, and place in a large bowl of ice water (to prevent sticking together). In a large Dutch oven, brown beef and sausage. Remove with a slotted spoon and reserve meats. Pour off all, but 3 tablespoons, of fat. Sauté onions and garlic in fat, until tender. Return meat to pan, and add tomatoes, spaghetti sauce, salt, pepper, and oregano; bring to a simmer, and simmer, over low heat, for 30 minutes; stir frequently (to prevent sticking). In a large bowl, beat eggs; add spinach, cottage cheese, and additional salt, to taste. Prepare the inside of casserole with butter; place 1 layer of noodles on bottom of pan. Next, add a layer of the spinach mixture; then, meat sauce. Then, add next Parmesan cheese; then, Mozzarella cheese. Repeat layers, until all ingredients have been used. Make top layer Mozzarella cheese. Bake at 350 degrees for 30 minutes.

Lemon Pound Cake with a "Twist"

- 1 box Yellow Pound Cake Mix
- 1 box Lemon Instant Pudding Mix
- 4 large eggs
- ⅓ cup oil (not olive oil)
- 1 cup water
- 2 tablespoons lemon juice

GLAZE

- 8 ounces confectioners' sugar
- 4 tablespoons lemon juice

(The "twist" is the light but tangy glaze.)

Preheat oven to 350 degrees. Mix all ingredients together; then, beat, at cake mix speed, for 2 minutes. Spray a Bundt cake pan lightly with Pam. Dust inside of cake pan with flour; tap pan gently, and pour out excess flour. Pour cake batter into the pan. Bake in middle of oven for 40 minutes or so. Test cake for doneness by pressing lightly with fingers. Cake should spring back immediately. Also, cake should have baked away from the sides of the pan. Remove from oven; allow to cool on rack for about 15 minutes. Invert on a cake plate or cake stand. Pour glaze over cake and allow to drizzle down sides and middle.

For the glaze: Put sugar and lemon juice in saucepan. Place saucepan over gentle heat. Stir mixture with a wooden spoon (stirring constantly), until mixture is smooth and coats the back of the spoon. (*It only takes a minute - do not overheat or overcook.) Immediately pour over the cake.

Haley - 4 years; and Shy, Jr. - 2 years

Jerry Jones, Jr. (left) with father - Jerry, and brother - Stephen

Biggest Challenge Ever Faced in Life

"The Texas Bar Examination." —*Jerry, Jr.*

If I Were Not in Professional Football I Would Be

"An attorney." —*Jerry, Jr.*

Three People I Would Invite to a "Fantasy" Dinner Party

"Abraham Lincoln, my maternal grandfather, and Socrates." —*Jerry, Jr.*

My Last Meal Would Be

"Chicken-fried steak, mashed potatoes, black-eyed peas, and green beans." —*Jerry, Jr.*

Jerry, Jr. (middle, front) with Jones family

Jerry Jones, Jr.

Dallas Cowboys
Front Office
Vice President /
Legal Operations

Philosophy to Live by

"The four 'P's': You must have a *plan*, it must have *priority*, you must stay *positive*, and you must *persevere*." — *Jerry, Jr.*

Jerry, Jr. (right) with sister - Charlotte (left), mother - Gene (middle), and Olympic gymnast, Kerri Strug (front)

BORN

9-27-69

COLLEGE

Georgetown & SMU (Juris Doctorate)

PETS

Fish (Aquarium)

Best Advice I Could Give to a High School Senior

"Dare to be great." —*Jerry, Jr.*

What I Value Most

"Family." —*Jerry, Jr.*

Best Asset

"A loving, caring family." —*Jerry, Jr.*

Favorite Childhood Snack
"Grilled cheese." —*Jerry, Jr.*

Favorite Holiday or Holiday Tradition
"Christmas Eve dinner." —*Jerry, Jr.*

Favorite City outside of Dallas
"Destin, Florida." —*Jerry, Jr.*

Hobbies and Other Interests
"Reading, hunting, and tennis." —*Jerry, Jr.*

Most Memorable Moment in Life outside of Pro-Football
"Passing the Texas Bar Exam." —*Jerry, Jr.*

Favorite Time of Day and Why
"When I've accomplished something." —*Jerry, Jr.*

Southwestern Omelet

1 tablespoon butter
1 medium white onion, chopped
1 green bell pepper, chopped
1 red bell pepper, chopped
mushrooms
4 egg whites
salsa
salt and pepper, to taste

Sauté onion, green pepper, and red pepper in butter, over medium heat, until peppers are tender and onions are translucent. Add mushrooms; sauté for a minute. Add egg whites; fold over when set. Serve topped with salsa. Salt and pepper, to taste.

Barry Switzer

Dallas Cowboys Football Club Head Coach

What I Value Most

"My children." — *Barry*

BORN

10-5-37

COLLEGE

Arkansas

CHILDREN

Greg - 29 years

Kathy - 28 years

Doug - 25 years

Barry Switzer's house (May, 1997): Dad (with Kathy behind) and Doug - on the new "Boy Toys"!

Hobbies and Other Interests

"Fishing, hunting, and riding my Harley." — *Barry*

Switzer family: Greg, Barry, Kathy, and Doug

Italian Eggs

1 bunch spring green onions
1 large can Progresso whole, peeled plum tomatoes
1 dozen eggs
olive oil (extra-virgin "First Cold Pressed")
Tabasco sauce
salt

Squash up tomatoes; put to side. Chop up onions; put in large skillet. Cover onions with olive oil; sauté onions (not too brown). When onions are almost brown, add squashed-up tomatoes. Cook about 15 minutes. While cooking, add salt and Tabasco sauce "to taste"; decrease heat, from high to medium/low, while sautéing. After about 15 minutes, turn heat to low setting. Crack eggs open on top of sauce (poaching style); then, cover and cook for 4 to 7 minutes (preference on whether you want runny or hard yolks).

Pasta Fagioli

(Fagioli = beans, in Italian)

1 pound white navy beans
1 small can Progresso whole, peeled plum tomatoes, mashed
3 stalks celery, chopped
6 cloves raw garlic, chopped (at least 6 or more)
½ cup extra-virgin "First Cold Pressed" olive oil
4 bay leaves
2 tablespoons salt (at least; add more, to taste)

Clean beans; soak in pot overnight. Cook beans, on low heat, covered, for 1 hour; cover with water (ex.: if beans are 2 inches high from bottom of pot, then add water at least 2 inches higher than the beans). After the beans cook, on low heat, for 1 hour, then add tomatoes, celery, garlic, olive oil, salt, and bay leaves. Cook, on low heat, for approximately another hour; taste beans - to tell when they're done.

To serve: Boil pasta; strain. Put pasta back into empty pot; then, scoop out some beans and add to pasta - "Pasta Fagioli"

Barry Switzer's children: Alaina (Greg's wife); Greg; Kathy; and Doug (Summer, 1996)

SUGAR
XX
SOAP
Tom Thumb
Reward

Players

Troy Kenneth Aikman

Philosophy to Live By

"The Golden Rule: 'Do unto others as you would have them do unto you.'" — *Troy*

Troy Aikman with family members - left to right: back row - Mike Powell and wife, Tammy (sister); Terri (sister) and husband, David Starns; Brooke Foreman (niece); and nephews - Drew Powell (left) and Brady Foreman

All-Pro Quarterback

6′4″
219 lbs.

BORN
11-21-66

COLLEGE
UCLA

YEARS IN NFL
9th Year
Dallas Cowboys

Best Advice I Could Give to a High School Senior

"Set goals and work towards them." — *Troy*

What I Value Most

"Friendships." — *Troy*

Best Asset

"Family and friends." — *Troy*

There's always a bunch of kids around Troy

If I Were Not in Professional Football I Would Be

"In some area of sports medicine (both of my sisters are nurses) - it's a field that helps people." — *Troy*

Three People I Would Invite to a "Fantasy" Dinner Party

"Elvis Presley, John F. Kennedy, and General George Patton." — *Troy*

Former Cowboys Player/Coach I Most Admire and Why

"Roger Staubach - because of what he has done both on and off the field." — *Troy*

Troy's favorite sport - second only to football!

Favorite Pre-Game or Post-Game Meal

"Pasta." — *Troy*

My Last Meal Would Be

"Pizza." — *Troy*

Favorite Childhood Snack

"Apple Jacks." — *Troy*

Favorite Holiday or Holiday Tradition

"Christmas." — *Troy*

Hobbies and Other Interests

"Golf." — *Troy*

Most Memorable Moment in Life outside of Pro-Football

"Watching my sisters graduate from college." — *Troy*

Favorite Time of Day and Why

"Sunset - just my favorite time." — *Troy*

Beef Supper

2 pounds beef for stew, cut in 1" cubes
2 large onions, sliced
2 tablespoons olive oil, or vegetable oil
1 jar (4½-ounce) of mushrooms, whole
4 medium-size potatoes, peeled and thinly-sliced
1 can (10½-ounce) cream of mushroom soup
¾ cup milk
¾ cup sour cream
1 teaspoon salt
¼ teaspoon pepper
2 cups shredded Cheddar cheese
cracker or fine dry bread crumbs

Season meat with salt and pepper. In a large skillet, cook and stir meat and onions in oil, over medium heat, until meat is brown and onions are tender; pour off oil. Save liquid from mushrooms; add enough water to make 1 cup. Stir mushrooms and liquid into meat mixture; heat to a boil. Reduce heat and cover; simmer for 2 hours. Heat oven to 350 degrees. Pour meat mixture into 13" x 9" baking dish. Arrange potatoes over meat mixture. Mix soup, milk, sour cream, salt, and pepper together; pour over potatoes. Sprinkle with cheese. Bake, uncovered, for 1 hour. Sprinkle with cracker crumbs, if desired. Bake, uncovered, until potatoes are tender (about 20 to 30 minutes).

Vegetable-Rice Casserole

2 cups cooked long-grain rice
1 package (10-ounce) frozen peas, cooked and drained
1 cup sour cream
1 cup diced celery
¼ cup minced onion
1 teaspoon curry powder (or, to taste)
½ teaspoon salt
½ teaspoon dry mustard

Preheat oven to 350 degrees. Butter 1-quart baking dish. Combine all ingredients in large bowl. Turn into dish; bake, until heated through (about 25 minutes). Serve immediately. Makes 4 servings.

Troy's Favorite Chocolate Chip Cookies

1 cup, plus 2 tablespoons, flour
½ teaspoon baking soda
½ teaspoon salt
½ cup butter, softened
6 tablespoons sugar
6 tablespoons packed brown sugar
1 teaspoon vanilla
1 egg
1 package (12-ounce) semi-sweet chocolate chips
1 cup nuts

Preheat oven to 375 degrees. In small bowl, combine flour, salt, and baking soda. In large bowl, combine butter, sugars, vanilla, and egg; mix well. Gradually add flour. Stir in chocolate chips and nuts. Using an ice-cream scoop (very important to use the scoop), put on ungreased cookie sheet. Bake 8 to 10 minutes. *Doesn't make many cookies, but they are large and delicious!!

Larry C., Jr. & Janelle Allen

73

All-Pro
Guard/Tackle

6'3"
326 lbs.

BORN

Larry - 11-27-71

Janelle - 5-7-71

COLLEGE

Larry - Sonoma State

YEARS IN NFL

4th Year

Dallas Cowboys

SPOUSE'S OCCUPATION

Homemaker

ANNIVERSARY

March 4 - 2 years

CHILDREN

Jayla Lee - 2 years

Larry, III - 1 year

Best Advice I Could Give to a High School Senior

"Work hard, and go to college and finish."—*Janelle*

Family picture taken for Mother's Day (1997) - left to right: Jayla, Larry, Larry III, and Janelle

What I Value Most

"Wife and kids." —*Larry*

"Husband and kids." —*Janelle*

Biggest Challenge Ever Faced in Life

"First game in NFL." —*Larry*

If I Were Not in Professional Football I Would Be

"Boxing." —*Larry*

Favorite Pre-Game or Post-Game Meal

"Steak." —*Larry*

Jayla (2½ years) and little Larry Allen (1 year)

My Last Meal Would Be

"Steak and French fries." *— Larry*

"Pizza." *—Janelle*

Favorite Childhood Snack

"Steak." *— Larry*

Favorite Holiday or Holiday Tradition

"Christmas." *— Larry and Janelle*

Favorite City outside of Dallas

"San Francisco, California" *— Larry and Janelle*

Hobbies and Other Interests

"Fishing and traveling." *— Larry*

"Shopping and traveling." *—Janelle*

Most Memorable Moment in Life outside of Pro-Football

"Wedding day, and the day the children were born." *— Larry*

"The day the children were born." *—Janelle*

Favorite Time of Day and Why

"Night - it's time to relax." *— Larry and Janelle*

Larry with Janelle - holding the fish he caught on their first fishing trip

Tamale Pie

1 dozen tamales, shucked
1 chicken (3 pounds), boiled, boned, and shredded
1 onion, chopped
1 clove garlic, minced
½ green pepper, chopped
olive oil, or vegetable oil
1 can (16-ounce) tomato sauce
1 can (4-ounce) can chopped ripe olives, drained
2 tablespoons chili powder
1 can (14-ounce) cream-style corn
½ pound Cheddar cheese, grated

Line a 13" x 9" casserole dish with tamales. Cover with a layer of chicken. Sauté onion, garlic, and pepper in oil; add to combined tomato sauce, olives, corn, and chili powder. Pour sauce over chicken; top with cheese. Bake at 300 degrees for 1 hour, or until cheese is bubbly.

Old-Fashioned Potato Soup

4 medium potatoes, diced
1 large onion, diced
½ cup celery, diced
1¼ cups water
3 cups milk
1 tablespoon salt
¼ teaspoon pepper
8 slices bacon, diced
2 tablespoons minced parsley

Combine potatoes, onion, celery, and water together. Cover; simmer for 45 minutes, or until done. Put vegetables through a course sieve; return to the water in which they were cooked. Add milk, salt, and pepper; reheat. Cook bacon until crisp. Just before serving, float parsley and crisp bacon pieces on top of soup.

Gingerbread

1 egg, beaten
½ cup sugar
½ cup light molasses
5 tablespoons butter, melted
⅔ cup cold water
1½ cups all-purpose flour
1 teaspoon baking soda
1 teaspoon ground ginger
½ teaspoon salt
whipped cream

Combine egg, sugar, molasses, butter, and water; mix well. In a large mixing bowl, stir together flour, baking soda, ginger, and salt; add molasses mixture. Beat, until well-mixed. Pour into a greased 8-inch square baking pan. Bake at 350 degrees for 30 minutes, or until cake tests done. Serve warm with whipped cream. Makes 9 servings.

Antonio Kenneth Anderson

96

Defensive Tackle

Philosophy to Live by

"The hard work you put in - the result will show from it." — *Antonio*

6'6"
318 lbs.

BORN

6-4-73

COLLEGE

Syracuse

YEARS IN NFL

Rookie

© James D. Smith Photography

Antonio Anderson - one of 14 children - has three cousins who have played pro sports

Best Advice I Could Give to a High School Senior

"Play hard - it could be the last chance playing ball." — *Antonio*

What I Value Most

"My family and friends." — *Antonio*

Best Asset

"Personality and charm." — *Antonio*

Biggest Challenge Ever Faced in Life

"Graduating from college." — *Antonio*

If I Were Not in Professional Football I Would Be

"Social worker." — *Antonio*

Three People I Would Invite to a "Fantasy" Dinner Party

"The President, Michael Jackson, and Wu-Tang Clan." — *Antonio*

Former Cowboys Player/Coach Most Admired & Why

"Leon Lett - the games' best defensive tackle." — *Antonio*

Game Day Rituals

"Listen to some Wu-Tang." — *Antonio*

Favorite Pre-Game or Post-Game Meal

Pre-Game - "Steak and egg, and spaghetti and meatballs." — *Antonio*

My Last Meal Would Be

"Triple-decker burger." — *Antonio*

Favorite Childhood Snack

"Now and Laters." — *Antonio*

Favorite Holiday or Holiday Tradition

"Christmas." — *Antonio*

Favorite City outside of Dallas

"New York City." — *Antonio*

Hobbies and Other Interests

"Playing play station, chess, and listening to rhythm and blues and rap." — *Antonio*

Favorite Time of Day and Why

"6 p.m. - end of the work day." — *Antonio*

Special Hamburgers

2 teaspoons salt
dash of pepper
2 pounds ground beef
6 onion slices, very thinly-sliced
6 bacon slices

Mix seasonings with ground beef. Divide ground beef to make 12 patties (about 4½ inches in diameter) for each burger. Place onion slice between two patties; seal edges of patties well. Wrap each patty with a bacon slice, fastened with toothpick. Grill each side for 6 to 7 minutes (for rare) and 9 to 10 minutes (for medium). Makes 6 patties.

Beefy Baked Beans

1½ pounds ground chuck
2 medium onions, chopped
½ stick butter
2 cans (20¾-ounce) pork and beans
3 cans (15-ounce) Ranch Style Beans
¼ cup prepared mustard
½ cup brown sugar
¼ cup syrup (prefer maple)
1 cup ketchup

Brown beef and onions in butter; add beans. Mix remaining ingredients; add to meat and beans. Place all in a casserole, or bean pot; refrigerate overnight. Bake at 300 degrees for 1½ hours.

*This recipe should be prepared 1 day in advance of baking.

William F. "Bill" & Denise Bates

All-Pro Safety

6'1"
213 lbs.

Philosophy to Live by

"Always do the very best you can at whatever you do - so that when you look back, you will have no regrets." — *Bill*

"What would Jesus do?" — *Denise*

The Bates "Bunch" at Busch Gardens (July, 1997)

BORN

Bill - 6-6-61

Denise - 1-25-60

COLLEGE

Bill - Tennessee

Denise - Tennessee

YEARS IN NFL

15th Year

Dallas Cowboys

SPOUSE'S OCCUPATION

Mom & business owner

ANNIVERSARY

June 8 - 12 years

CHILDREN

Graham, Brianna, & Hunter - 8 years

Tanner - 6 years

Dillon - 2 years

PETS

Blitz - Rottweiler

2 hamsters

saltwater fish

Best Advice I Could Give to a High School Senior

"Respect your parents and coaches, choose your friends carefully, and do the right thing." — *Bill*

"Do the best you can - your actions and grades reflect who you are!" — *Denise*

What I Value Most

"My wife, my family, and my faith." — *Bill*

"My husband, my children, and my belief in God." — *Denise*

Best Asset

"Determination." — *Bill*

"Being involved." — *Denise*

Bill Bates and daughter, Brianna (8 years old), "Daddy's Little Girl" - Brianna was a flower girl at a wedding in April, 1997

Biggest Challenge Ever Faced in Life

"Making the Dallas Cowboys team as an undrafted free agent." — *Bill*

"Delivering triplets!" — *Denise*

If I Were Not in Professional Football I Would Be

"A professional golfer." — *Bill*

Three People I Would Invite to a "Fantasy" Dinner Party

"Mel Gibson, Jim Carey, and David Letterman." — *Bill*

Former Cowboys Player/Coach Most Admired and Why

"Tom Landry - for his beliefs and stability as a person." — *Bill*

"Bob Breunig - for the hospitality that he and his wife showed to the other players, and his helping so many others." — *Denise*

Game Day Rituals

"Rest up to game time, call my wife before the game, and stretch a certain way." — *Bill*

"Usually entertaining company - then arriving at least one hour before game time." — *Denise*

Favorite Pre-Game or Post-Game Meal

Post-Game - "Cheeseburger and fries." — *Bill*

Denise and Dillon (2 years old)
"Western Night" at family camp (June, 1997)

My Last Meal Would Be

"Prime rib." — *Bill*

"Salad, pasta, and ice cream." — *Denise*

Favorite Childhood Snack

"Sweet Tarts." — *Bill*

"Popcorn and coke." — *Denise*

left to right: Dillon, Tanner, Hunter, Brianna, and Graham Bates
in Maui (March, 1997)

Favorite Holiday or Holiday Tradition

"Christmas." — *Bill*

"Thanksgiving—because that's when all my family comes to visit." — *Denise*

Favorite City outside of Dallas

"Knoxville, Tennessee." — *Bill*

"Nashville, Tennessee." — *Denise*

Hobbies and Other Interests

"Golf, ranching, and more golf." — *Bill*

"Tennis, photography, computers, and interior design." — *Denise*

Most Memorable Moment in Life outside of Pro-Football

"Meeting my wife." — *Bill*

"Giving birth." — *Denise*

Favorite Time of Day and Why

"Morning - to get ready to take on another day." — *Bill*

"Late evening - the kids are in bed, and the house is quiet!" — *Denise*

Bill - with three sons at football camp (June, 1997) - left to right: Tanner (6 years); Graham (8 years); and Hunter (8 years)

Breakfast Burritos

1 pound sausage
flour tortillas
1 onion, chopped
½ pound Velveeta cheese, cubed
6 to 8 eggs, beaten

Brown sausage and onion; drain grease. Add Velveeta and eggs. When Velveeta is melted, stir until eggs are done. Warm tortillas. Serve egg mixture on the tortillas.

Chicken & Dumplings

CHICKEN BROTH
2 chickens (3 to 4 pounds)
2 to 3 onions, quartered
4 to 6 carrots, quartered
6 to 8 celery stalks with leaves, halved
2 to 3 bay leaves
10 to 12 peppercorns, crushed
2 teaspoons dried thyme
2 teaspoons garlic powder
1 to 2 tablespoons salt

DUMPLINGS
3 cups unsifted all-purpose flour
½ teaspoon salt
½ cup shortening
⅔ cup, plus 1 tablespoon, ice water

In a large pot, combine chicken and all broth ingredients. Heat to boiling, reduce heat, and simmer for at least 4 hours; drain. Remove chicken, and cool. Remove skin and bones. Skim fat from broth. Combine flour and salt for dumplings; cut in shortening. Add water (slowly), until dough adheres together. Divide in half or quarters. Roll out each on a floured surface to ⅛" (or thinner, as you prefer). Cut into 1" x 2" strips. Drop into boiling broth; stir. Reduce heat. Cover, and simmer about 20 minutes, until done. Add chicken. Ready to serve!

Chicken Salad

4 chicken breasts, cooked and cut up
1 box Rice-a-Roni chicken-flavored rice (can use Uncle Ben's)
2 jars (6-ounce) marinated artichoke hearts
1 cup mayonnaise
green olives, sliced

Prepare chicken and rice (according to package directions); mix well together. Cut up artichoke hearts, reserving juice. Add artichokes. Mix the artichoke juice with the mayonnaise; set aside. Cut up olives into slices (about 12 to 15 olives); add olives. Pour juice from artichoke hearts and mayonnaise mixture over the mixed chicken and rice, artichokes, and olives; mix well. Stir several times before serving. Refrigerate overnight for best flavor. Garnish with olives, if desired. Enjoy!

Denise and Bill Bates with their children - in Crested Butte, Colorado (February, 1997)

Darren & Teresa Benson

Defensive Tackle

6'7"
308 lbs.

Best Advice I Could Give to a High School Senior

"The world is yours." — *Darren*

Darren Benson - in action against the Philadelphia Eagles

BORN

Darren - 8-25-74

COLLEGE

Darren - Trinity Valley Community College

Teresa - Trinity Valley Community College

SPOUSE'S OCCUPATION

Housewife & college student

ANNIVERSARY

February 17 - 1 year

YEARS IN NFL

3rd Year

Dallas Cowboys

Philosophy to Live by

"Stick with your dreams, and you'll go far." — *Darren*

What I Value Most

"My parents." — *Darren*

Biggest Challenge Ever Faced in Life

"Wanting to give up on football after my first year." — *Darren*

If I Were Not in Professional Football I Would Be
"A construction worker - like my father." *—Darren*

Three People I Would Invite to a "Fantasy" Dinner Party
"Reggie White, Richard Dent, and Dick Butkus." *—Darren*

Former Cowboys Player/Coach Most Admired and Why
"John Blake - he stuck with me my first year." *—Darren*

Game Day Rituals
"Think the whole game out in my mind." *—Darren*

My Last Meal Would Be
"Big steak and potatoes." *—Darren*

Favorite Childhood Snack
"All junk food." *—Darren*

Favorite Holiday or Holiday Tradition
"Christmas - no school for weeks." *—Darren*

Favorite City outside of Dallas
"Memphis, Tennessee." *—Darren*

Hobbies and Other Interests
"Music, and time to myself." *—Darren*

Most Memorable Moment in Life outside of Pro-Football
"Graduating from school." *—Darren*

Favorite Time of Day and Why
"9:00 p.m. - it's the end of the day, and time to relax and sleep." *—Darren*

Rotel Chicken

1 hen (5-pound)
2 large green peppers, chopped
2 large onions, chopped
1½ sticks butter
1 package (7-ounce) vermicelli
1 can (10-ounce) Rotel tomatoes
2 tablespoons Worcestershire sauce
1 can (17-ounce) tiny English peas, drained
1 can (8-ounce) mushrooms, drained
2 pounds Velveeta cheese, cut up
salt and pepper, to taste

Season and bake hen in enough water so that you will have ½ to 1 quart broth in which to cook vermicelli. Cook hen, according to size. Chop and sauté green pepper and onions in butter. Cook vermicelli in chicken broth. When almost done, add Rotel tomatoes (mashed), but only one-half the juice. Add Worcestershire sauce, sautéed onions, and peppers; cool together, until it begins to thicken. Add peas, mushrooms, and cheese. When cheese has melted, add chicken that has been cut to desired size. Season, to taste, with salt and pepper. Cook, uncovered, in 2 casserole dishes (2½-quart) at 325 degrees, until bubbly.

Eggnog Pie

1 envelope unflavored gelatin
¼ cup cold water
¾ cup sugar
1 tablespoon cornstarch
¼ teaspoon salt
2 eggs, separated
1½ cups milk
1 tablespoon, plus 1 teaspoon, vanilla
1 teaspoon ground nutmeg
¼ cup sugar
1 baked 9-inch pie crust
1 cup whipping cream, whipped
candied pineapples and cherries, diced
ground nutmeg

Soften gelatin in cold water; set aside. Combine ¾ cup sugar, cornstarch, and salt in a heavy saucepan. Combine egg yolks and milk; beat well, and add to mixture in saucepan. Cook milk mixture, over medium heat, stirring constantly, until mixture begins to boil; boil 1 minute. Remove from heat; add gelatin mixture. Stir, until gelatin granules dissolve. Stir in vanilla and 1 teaspoon nutmeg. Let custard mixture cool, until the consistency of unbeaten egg white. Beat egg whites (at room temperature), until soft peaks form; gradually add ¼ cup sugar (1 tablespoon at a time), beating until stiff peaks form and sugar dissolves. Fold egg whites into custard. Pour filling into baked pie crust. Chill at least 8 hours. Spoon whipped cream in a ring over the pie. Arrange candied fruit on top of whipped cream; sprinkle lightly with nutmeg. Makes one 9-inch pie.

Eric Bjornson

86

Tight End

6′4″
236 lbs.

BORN
12-15-71

COLLEGE
Washington

YEARS IN NFL
3rd Year
Dallas Cowboys

PETS
Fletch -
Golden Retriever

Best Advice I Could Give to a High School Senior

"Work extremely hard to achieve your goals, but don't forget to have fun." —Eric

Eric and Brooke (girl friend) - in Hawaii (March, 1997)

What I Value Most

"My family." —*Eric*

Best Asset

"Sense of humor." —*Eric*

If I Were Not in Professional Football I Would Be

"Looking for a job." —*Eric*

Favorite Time of Day and Why

"Just before the sun goes down." —*Eric*

Eric - at his sister's wedding in June, 1997 -
left to right: Eric; Kristen (sister); Laurie (sister),
with new husband, Scott; Sharon (mom); and Tom (dad)

Three People I Would Invite to a "Fantasy" Dinner Party

"Dave Letterman, Eddie Vedder, and Larry Bird." —*Eric*

Favorite Pre-Game or Post-Game Meal

"Pasta." —*Eric*

My Last Meal Would Be

"Pizza." —*Eric*

Favorite Holiday or Holiday Tradition

"Christmas." —*Eric*

Favorite City outside of Dallas

"Seattle, Washington." —*Eric*

Hobbies and Other Interests

"Golf, and movies." —*Eric*

Bow-Tie Pasta

6 to 8 tablespoons olive oil (or more)
5 garlic cloves, minced
10 small (or 6 large) tomatoes, chopped
1 block Mozzarella cheese, chopped into small squares
1 package Feta cheese (or Blue cheese), crumbled
1 can olives, chopped
fresh basil, broken up
1½ pounds bow-tie pasta

Put all of the ingredients together in a large bowl, except for the pasta. Marinate for at least an hour or, even better, overnight. Cook pasta; add to bowl.

* Optional: May add any additional vegetables (broccoli or spinach recommended)

Eric - with new puppy, "Fletch"

Bob & Mary Breunig

Supporting the children at

Happy Hill Farm

Academy/Home

since 1978

Macey Brooks

Wide Receiver

6′5″
220 lbs.

BORN
2-2-75

COLLEGE
James Madison

YEARS IN NFL
Rookie

Philosophy to Live by

"Try to make everyone you come in contact with smile - it's free." — *Macey*

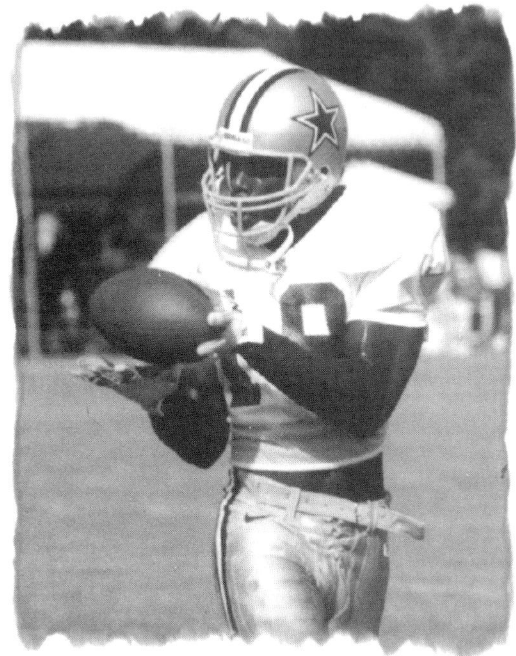

Macey Brooks - the first James Madison University player to be drafted by the Cowboys

Best Advice I Could Give to a High School Senior

"Listen to your heart and your parents." — *Macey*

What Do You Value Most

"My family." — *Macey*

Best Asset

"Sense of humor - it goes a long way!" — *Macey*

Biggest Challenge Ever Faced in Life
"Life itself." — *Macey*

If I Were Not in Professional Football I Would Be
"In school." — *Macey*

Three People I Would Invite to a "Fantasy" Dinner Party
"Mother, father, and Jesus." — *Macey*

Former Cowboys Player/Coach Most Admired and Why
"Billy Bates - because of the perseverance he's shown." — *Macey*

Game Day Rituals
"Prayer in far end zone after coming out of tunnel." — *Macey*

My Last Meal Would Be
"Fried pork chops, mashed potatoes, and cream corn." — *Macey*

Favorite Childhood Snack
"Root beer float." — *Macey*

Brooks - (number 19 during the preseaseason) has great size and ability - not only to protect the ball from opposing defenders, but also to be an effective blocker

Favorite Holiday or Holiday Tradition

"Christmas." — *Macey*

Favorite City outside of Dallas

"San Francisco, California." — *Macey*

Hobbies and Other Interests

"Cooking, eating, fishing, and golf." — *Macey*

Favorite Time of Day and Why

"12 p.m. - because "Days of Our Lives" comes on." — *Macey*

Spanish Rice

1 tablespoon bacon drippings
¾ cup long-grain white rice
½ cup chopped onion
1 garlic clove, minced
3 small canned tomatoes, diced
2 tablespoons tomato juice
2 cups hot water
½ teaspoon salt

In a skillet, heat, on medium-high, bacon drippings. Add rice; cook, and stir, until rice is golden brown. Add onion and garlic; stir, and cook 3 additional minutes. Add all remaining ingredients. Cook, uncovered, on medium heat, for 20 minutes, stirring only once after 10 minutes. Check rice for doneness by tasting a few of the top grains. If rice is firm, add a little more water; cover, and cook 5 minutes more. Makes 6 servings.

Almond Danish

1 cup butter, softened
2 packages dry yeast
½ cup warm water
⅓ cup sugar, divided
¾ cup milk
2 eggs
4½ cups all-purpose flour, divided
1 teaspoon salt
1 egg, beaten
sugar
¼ cup sliced almonds

FILLING

1 can (8-ounce) almond paste, crumbled
½ cup butter, softened
½ cup sugar

Place 2 sticks butter, 1 inch apart, between 2 sheets of wax paper; roll into a 12-inch square; place on cookie sheet, and chill, until ready to use. In a large bowl, dissolve yeast in warm water; add ½ teaspoon sugar, and let stand 5 minutes. Add remaining sugar, milk, 2 eggs, 3 cups flour, and salt; beat, at medium speed of electric mixer, 3 minutes. Stir in enough flour to make soft dough; cover, and chill 30 minutes. Place dough on a lightly-floured surface; roll into 18" x 13" rectangle. Peel top sheet of wax paper from butter; place butter on one end of dough to cover two-thirds of the dough. Peel off remaining wax paper from butter. Fold uncovered third of dough over middle third; fold remaining third over middle third. Turn dough clockwise so open end is away from you. Roll dough into a 24" x 12" rectangle. Fold ends to center; then, fold dough in half. Turn dough so open side is away from you. Repeat rolling/folding procedure twice; cover, and chill dough 1 hour. Divide dough in half. Place half of dough on lightly-floured surface; refrigerate unused portion. Roll dough into a 30" x 9" rectangle; cut lengthwise into 3 strips. Spread about ¼ cup of Almond Filling evenly down center of each strip; fold edges of strips over filling, and seal. Place 3 ropes, side by side, on large ungreased baking sheet; braid. Join ends of dough to make a 9-inch ring. Repeat procedure with remaining dough and filling; let rise in a warm place, free from drafts, for 45 minutes, or until doubled in bulk. Brush with beaten egg; sprinkle with sugar and almonds. Bake at 350 degrees for 25 to 30 minutes, until golden. Cool on wire racks. Makes 2 coffee cakes.

For Almond Filling: Combine all ingredients in a bowl; beat, at medium speed of an electric mixer, until well-blended. Makes 1⅔ cups.

Shante Carver

Defensive End

6′5″
253 lbs.

BORN
2-12-71

COLLEGE
Arizona

YEARS IN NFL
4th Year
Dallas Cowboys

PETS
Rowdy and Sam - Dogs

Philosophy to Live by

"Live one day, one hour, and one minute at a time." — *Shante*

Shante Carver - spent his first two years in pro-football working under and learning from Charles Haley and Tony Tolbert

Best Advice I Could Give to a High School Senior

"Go to school and get your education." — *Shante*

What I Value Most

"My family and good friends." — *Shante*

Best Asset

"Good with people." — *Shante*

Shante - a versatile defender for the Cowboys in 1997

Biggest Challenge Ever Faced in Life

"Overcoming my mom's death and flunking out of school at the same time." — *Shante*

If I Were Not in Professional Football I Would Be

"An educator of some kind." — *Shante*

Three People I Would Invite to a "Fantasy" Dinner Party

"Martin Kidd, Jimi Hendrix, and Bob Marley." — *Shante*

Game Day Rituals

"Just focus with music." — *Shante*

Favorite Pre-Game or Post-Game Meal

"Steak." — *Shante*

My Last Meal Would Be

"Steak and shrimp." — *Shante*

Favorite Childhood Snack

"Mayonnaise sandwich." — *Shante*

Favorite City outside of Dallas

"San Diego, California." — *Shante*

Hobbies and Other Interests

"Fishing, and traveling." — *Shante*

Favorite Time of Day and Why

"Night time - I can relax." — *Shante*

Cauliflower Bake

1 large cauliflower, cut into flowerets
½ teaspoon salt
3 cups water
¼ cup butter, melted
1 tablespoon sugar
½ teaspoon salt
½ teaspoon pepper
1 cup round buttery cracker crumbs
1½ cups shredded Cheddar cheese, divided
1 medium onion, chopped
½ cup chopped green bell pepper
1 can (16-ounce) whole tomatoes, undrained and chopped

In a large saucepan, combine cauliflower, salt, and water; bring to a boil. Cover, reduce heat, and cook for 5 minutes, or until tender; drain. Set aside. In a large bowl, combine butter, sugar, salt, pepper, and cracker crumbs; stir in cauliflower, 1 cup cheese, onion, bell pepper, and tomatoes. Spoon into lightly-greased individual baking dishes. Bake at 350 degrees for 20 to 25 minutes. Sprinkle with remaining ½ cup cheese; bake for 5 minutes more. Makes 6 servings.

* Casserole may be baked in a 13" x 9" x 2" baking dish at 350 degrees for 35 minutes; add remaining ½ cup cheese, and bake for 5 minutes more.

Boy, What We Can Learn

Look into their big, bright eyes and you'll see nothing but curiosity and innocence. Their ability to learn is infinite; their capacity to love, larger than life itself. They're excited by a bird, a butterfly, the moon, a piece of paper blowing in the wind or water dripping from a leaky faucet.

They're so happy with just a hug and kiss. When they don't question the person's religion, financial status, sexual preference or political views. They give so much and ask nothing.

Maybe if we could see things through their eyes for just a couple of minutes we'd try to make this world a better place for them to grow up in. Sometimes it's hard to believe we all started out as children.

Boy, what we can learn from them . . .

Kathy Ramarui

P.O. Box 630227
Irving, TX 75063
972/506-9044
972/506-9005 (fax)

Tony & Tamara Casillas

Defensive Tackle

6′3″
278 lbs.

Philosophy to Live by

"Play hard, and live life to the fullest—life is short." — *Tony*

"Treat everyone the way you wish to be treated." — *Tamara*

Chase's third birthday (Tamara, Chase, and Tony)

BORN

Tony - 10-26-63

Tamara - 9-1-61

COLLEGE

Tony - Oklahoma

Tamara - Ohio State

YEARS IN NFL

12th Year

Dallas Cowboys (5)

Atlanta Falcons (5)

New York Jets (2)

SPOUSE'S OCCUPATION

Homemaker

ANNIVERSARY

February 14 - newlyweds

CHILDREN

Chase - 3 years

PETS

Chavez - Rottweiler

Miss Marilyn Monroe - Maltese

Tex - Himalayan

Best Advice I Could Give to a High School Senior

"Enjoy your moment. Don't get in a hurry to speed up maturity." — *Tony*

"Prepare for and go to college." — *Tamara*

What I Value Most

"My family and life." — *Tony*

"My family." — *Tamara*

Best Asset

"Sensitivity." — *Tony*

"My ability to laugh at myself." — *Tamara*

Tony and Tamara's wedding -
in Los Cabos, Mexico, with friends and family

Biggest Challenge Ever Faced in Life

"Fatherhood." — *Tony*

"Managing thirteen people - many of whom were older than myself." — *Tamara*

If I Were Not in Professional Football I Would Be

"Aspiring to become an actor (bilingual)." — *Tony*

Three People I Would Invite to a "Fantasy" Dinner Party

"Robin Williams, Billy Crystal, and Eddie Murphy." — *Tony*

Former Cowboys Player/Coach Most Admired and Why

"Randy White - no nonsense, intense player; and Jimmy Johnson - winning attitude." — *Tony*

"Roger Staubach - he has always handled his fame with style and grace, and he continues to help worthy causes." — *Tamara*

Game Day Rituals

"Meditate for fifteen minutes, followed by fifteen-minute power nap." — *Tony*

"Church, wish Tony luck, field telephone calls, get dressed, say a prayer, and go." — *Tamara*

Favorite Pre-Game or Post-Game Meal

"Fruit/pancakes or French toast." — *Tony*

My Last Meal Would Be

"Mexican - Choriza, enchiladas, tortillas, beans, and rice." — *Tony*

"Roast, mashed potatoes, gravy, corn, rolls with real butter — what calories?" — *Tamara*

Favorite Childhood Snack

"Anything period (no buttermilk)." — *Tony*

"Anything chocolate." — *Tamara*

Favorite Holiday or Holiday Tradition

"Thanksgiving." — *Tony*

"Christmas." — *Tamara*

Favorite City outside of Dallas

"Pebble Beach, California, and Los Angeles, California." — *Tony*

"Los Angeles, California." — *Tamara*

Tony - takes a swing at Pebble Beach, California

Hobbies and Other Interests

"Golf, reading, sunbathing, and traveling." — *Tony*

"Roller blading, working out, golf, reading, and swimming." — *Tamara*

Most Memorable Moment in Life outside of Pro-Football

"Shooting (69 score) at St. Iuis Country Club." — *Tony*

"The birth of my son, Chase." — *Tamara*

Favorite Time of Day and Why

"Morning - just another day to thank God for living." — *Tony*

"Sunset - the best time to reflect on the blessings of the day."— *Tamara*

Limeade Grilled Chicken

MARINADE

1/3 cup Worcestershire sauce
1 can (6-ounce) frozen limeade concentrate, thawed
1½ teaspoons seasoned pepper
1 teaspoon finely-chopped, fresh garlic

CHICKEN

6 (4 ounces each) boneless, skinless chicken breasts

In large resealable plastic food bag, combine all marinade ingredients; add chicken. Tightly seal bag; turn bag over several times (to coat chicken well). Place in 13" x 9" pan. Refrigerate for 8 hours, or overnight.

Prepare grill; heat, until coals are ash-white. With slotted spoon, remove chicken from marinade; save marinade. Place chicken on grill; brush with marinade. Cover; grill, basting with marinade. Turn, occasionally, until chicken is fork-tender (35 to 45 minutes).

* Note: Fat is only 2 grams!

Spring Primavera

½ pound uncooked fettucini or spaghetti
½ pound asparagus, trimmed and cut into 1-inch pieces
1 small red or green pepper, cut into short thin strips
1½ cups shredded carrots
2 garlic cloves, finely-chopped
1½ teaspoons Italian herb seasoning, crushed
2 tablespoons olive or vegetable oil
¼ cup grated Parmesan cheese

Cook fettucini, as package directs; drain. Cook and stir asparagus, bell pepper, carrots, garlic, and herb seasoning in skillet in hot oil, over medium-high heat, for 3 to 5 minutes, or until tender-crisp. Remove from heat. Stir in fettucine and cheese. Serve immediately. Makes 4 servings.

Dexter Coakley

Linebacker

5'10"
215 lbs.

BORN
10-20-72

COLLEGE
Appalachian State

YEARS IN NFL
Rookie

Philosophy to Live by

"Pray for the things you need, and work for those things that you want." — *Dexter*

Dexter Coakley - has excellent speed and quickness, and is an impressive solid hitter

Best Advice I Could Give to a High School Senior

"Hard work pays off." — *Dexter*

What I Value Most

"Waking up every morning with good health and strength - life." — *Dexter*

Best Asset

"My ability to adapt." — *Dexter*

Biggest Challenge Ever Faced in Life

"Overcoming the stereotype that I was too short to make it at this level." — *Dexter*

If I Were Not in Professional Football I Would Be

"Working in broadcasting." —*Dexter*

Three People I Would Invite to a "Fantasy" Dinner Party

"Dick Butkus, Mike Singletary, and Sam Mills." —*Dexter*

Former Cowboys Player/Coach Most Admired & Why

"Tony Dorsett - because he accepted the challenge every time he stepped onto the field." —*Dexter*

Game Day Rituals

"Praying." —*Dexter*

Favorite Pre-Game or Post-Game Meal

"Skinless chicken breast." —*Dexter*

© James D. Smith Photography

Coakley - signs autographs for the fans at training camp

My Last Meal Would Be

"Pasta." —*Dexter*

Favorite Childhood Snack

"Little Debbie Cakes." —*Dexter*

Favorite Holiday or Holiday Tradition

"Christmas." —*Dexter*

Favorite City outside of Dallas
"Atlanta, Georgia." — *Dexter*

Hobbies and Other Interests
"Salt-water fishing with my dad." — *Dexter*

Most Memorable Moment in Life outside of Pro-Football
"Getting my college degree, and getting drafted by America's team." — *Dexter*

Favorite Time of Day and Why
"Morning - another chance to go out and prove myself and accept those challenges put forth before me." — *Dexter*

Special Cookies

1 cup butter	½ cup flaked coconut
1 cup sugar	1 cup chopped pecans
1 cup brown sugar	3½ cups flour
1 egg	1 teaspoon soda
1 cup oil	1 teaspoon salt
1 cup rolled oats	1 teaspoon vanilla
1 cup crushed cornflakes	powdered sugar

Preheat oven to 325 degrees. Cream butter and sugars, until light and fluffy. Add eggs; blend. Add oil, stirring, until oil is well-blended. Add oats, cornflakes, coconut, and pecans; stir, until well-mixed. Add flour, baking soda, salt, and vanilla; mix well. Form into balls (about the size of a walnut). Place on an ungreased cookie sheet; flatten with a fork dipped in water. Bake for 12 minutes. Allow to cool a few minutes before removing from pan. Sprinkle with powdered sugar. Makes 8 dozen.

Chicken with Cucumbers in Paprika Sauce

2 cucumbers, peeled and cut into ¼-inch slices
4 chicken breasts, skinless and boned, cut into strips
2 tablespoons paprika, divided
6 tablespoons butter
2 tablespoons oil
1 small onion, finely-diced
4 ounces white wine
1 pint whipping cream
salt and pepper, to taste
lemon juice
Worcestershire sauce

Blanch cucumbers in 2 quarts of boiling salt water; remove. Refresh cucumbers in cold water. Season chicken strips with salt and 1 teaspoon paprika. Melt butter in skillet; add oil. Allow to start browning; add diced onion. Stir; add chicken and brown on all sides. Remove chicken from skillet, and keep warm. Add paprika; cook for 2 minutes, over moderate heat. Add white wine; reduce by half. Add whipping cream; reduce until thick. Season with salt, pepper, lemon juice, and Worcestershire sauce, to taste; add chicken and cucumbers. Serve immediately. Makes 4 servings.

Richie & Kristin Cunningham

Kicker

5'10"
167 lbs.

BORN

Richie - 8-18-70

Kristin - 3-17-71

COLLEGE

Richie - Southwestern Louisiana

SPOUSE'S OCCUPATION

Speech pathologist

ANNIVERSARY

July 5 (newlyweds)

YEARS IN NFL

1st Year

Dallas Cowboys

Philosophy to Live by

"Live your dreams." — *Richie*

"To help others, and to live life to its fullest potential." — *Kristin*

Richie and Kristin Cunningham

Best Advice I Could Give to a High School Senior

"Strive to be the best in whatever you're called to do." — *Richie*

"Never give up, and it never hurts to try." — *Kristin*

What I Value Most

"Family and friends." — *Richie*

"Family, friends, and health." — *Kristin*

Best Asset

"Having great friends and a wonderful wife, who is a best friend." — *Richie*

"Being surrounded by wonderful people." — *Kristin*

Biggest Challenge Ever Faced in Life

"Live it each day - to be a good Christian." — *Richie*

"Completing college and graduate school." — *Kristin*

© James D. Smith Photography

Richie Cunningham - after a very competitive '97 training camp, was chosen as the kicker for this year's Dallas Cowboys team

If I Were Not in Professional Football I Would Be

"In the health-care industry." — *Richie*

Two People I Would Invite to a "Fantasy" Dinner Party

"Jimmy Buffet and Oprah Winfrey." — *Richie*

Former Cowboys Player/Coach Most Admired and Why

"Walt Garrison - he always seemed to have fun playing the game." — *Richie*

Game Day Rituals

"Meditating—kicking the perfect field goal throughout the day." — *Richie*

"Being nervous." — *Kristin*

Favorite Pre-Game or Post-Game Meal

"Steak and potatoes." — *Richie*

My Last Meal Would Be

"A big crawfish boil with family and friends." — *Richie*

"Lobster." — *Kristin*

Favorite Childhood Snack

"Cheese and crackers." — *Richie*

"Popsicles." — *Kristin*

Favorite Holiday or Holiday Tradition

"Christmas Eve - wearing matching pajamas at the O'Leary's home on Christmas Eve." — *Richie*

"Opening gifts, one at a time, to see everyone else's joy." — *Kristin*

Favorite City outside of Dallas

"San Diego, California." — *Richie*

"Boston, Massachusetts." — *Kristin*

Hobbies and Other Interests

"Golf, sailing, fishing, and hunting." — *Richie*

"Horseback riding, running, soccer, and tennis." — *Kristin*

Most Memorable Moment in Life outside of Pro-Football

"Marrying my wife/husband." — *Richie and Kristin*

Favorite Time of Day and Why

"Evening - time of the day when we slow down and relax." — *Richie*

"When the sun goes down - very romantic!" — *Kristin*

Mr. C's Seafood Gumbo
(Dad's Recipe)

1 pound okra
1 large onion, diced
¼ cup cooking oil
2 pounds shrimp
1 pound crab claw meat
½ clove garlic, crushed
red pepper or black pepper, to taste
salt, to taste

This is prepared best in large magna-light pot. Add diced onions to cooking oil. Sauté onions to a medium brown (be careful not to burn). Add okra; brown, and then pour 1 cup of water in pot. Cover, and smother okra for one-half hour, on a medium heat (add water as needed). After okra is smothered, add shrimp and garlic with another cup of water. Cook for 10 minutes, on a medium heat; stir as needed. Finally, add crab claw meat, along with 4 cups of water. At this time, add salt and pepper, to taste, along with filet seasoning, if available. Serve over rice.

William Augusta "Billy" Davis, III

Wide Receiver

6'1"
205 lbs.

Best Advice I Could Give to a High School Senior

"Believe; believe; and believe." — *Billy*

Billy Davis - has great competitiveness and the desire to be an outstanding wide receiver for the Cowboys

BORN

7-6-72

COLLEGE

Pittsburgh

YEARS IN NFL

3rd Year

Dallas Cowboys

PETS

Biggie - Black Sharpei

Philosophy to Live by

"Always set a standard higher than your adversary." — *Billy*

What I Value Most

"My faith, and my mother." — *Billy*

Best Asset

"Kindness." — *Billy*

Biggest Challenge Ever Faced in Life

"Being responsible, and my sister's illness." — *Billy*

If I Were Not in Professional Football I Would Be

"An actor." — *Billy*

Game Day Rituals

"Prayer." — *Billy*

Potato-Cheddar Cheese Soup

2 tablespoons butter
⅓ cup chopped celery
⅓ cup chopped onion
4 cups diced, peeled potatoes
3 cups chicken broth
2 cups milk
1½ teaspoons salt
¼ teaspoon pepper
dash of paprika
2 cups shredded Cheddar cheese
croutons
fresh, chopped parsley

In a large saucepan, over medium-high heat, melt butter; sauté celery and onion, until tender. Add potatoes and broth; cover, and simmer, until potatoes are tender. Pureé potato mixture in a blender or food processor (a little at a time); return to saucepan. Stir in milk and seasonings. Add cheese; heat only until melted. Garnish with croutons and parsley. Makes 8 servings.

Honey Crunch Cookies

2 cups all-purpose flour
2 teaspoons baking powder
½ teaspoon salt
1 cup butter
1 cup honey
2 eggs
1 cup shredded coconut
1 cup butterscotch chips
4 cups crisp rice cereal

Sift together flour, baking powder, and salt; set aside. In a large mixing bowl, cream butter; add honey (a little at a time); mix well. Add eggs (one at a time), beating well after each addition (mixture will appear to separate). Gradually add dry ingredients; mix, until moistened. Fold in coconut, butterscotch chips, and rice cereal. Drop by teaspoonfuls on greased cookie sheets. Bake at 350 degrees for about 12 minutes, or until golden brown. Remove cookies to cooling rack. Makes about 5 dozen.

Favorite City outside of Dallas

"New York City." — *Billy*

Hobbies and Other Interests

"Acting, modeling, and writing." — *Billy*

Our Mission

The Mission of the Dallas Cowboys Wives' Association (DCWA) is to maximize the potential of our group for excellence by positively impacting our community. We are committed to reflecting a positive image for the Dallas Cowboys, to offering a forum to promote unity among the players' wives, and to providing the opportunity for encouragement and support to various charitable organizations.

Wendell H. Davis

Cornerback

5'10"
183 lbs.

BORN
6-27-73

COLLEGE
Oklahoma

YEARS IN NFL
2nd Year
Dallas Cowboys

CHILDREN
Ashley - 7 years

Philosophy to Live by

"Do to others as you want done to you." — *Wendell*

Wendell Davis - finished second among rookies in special teams tackles in 1996

Best Advice I Could Give to a High School Senior

"Set a goal and work hard toward it - keep it in sight." — *Wendell*

What I Value Most

"Life, good health, and love." — *Wendell*

Best Asset

"1996 GMC Yukon truck." — *Wendell*

Biggest Challenge Ever Faced in Life

"Being a good NFL football player." — *Wendell*

If I Were Not in Professional Football I Would Be

"A football coach, or in the field of sociology (my major)." — *Wendell*

Three People I Would Invite to a "Fantasy" Dinner Party

"Mrs. F. Davis, Mr. W. Davis, and Coach Becker (high school coach)." — *Wendell*

Former Cowboys Player/Coach Most Admired & Why

"Barry Switzer (former University of Oklahoma Coach) - was head coach the year before I began playing at O. U. I met him and his family. It's nice to have him as my head coach with the Dallas Cowboys." — *Wendell*

Game Day Rituals

"To play the best I can with my whole heart." — *Wendell*

Favorite Pre-Game or Post-Game Meal

"Eggs, sausage, toast, and hash browns." — *Wendell*

Favorite Childhood Snack

"Apples and bananas." — *Wendell*

Favorite Holiday or Holiday Tradition

"Every day is special to me." — *Wendell*

Most Memorable Moment in Life outside of Pro-Football

"The day I signed my college scholarship at my graduation with friends and family." — *Wendell*

Favorite Time of Day and Why

"Any time after a game - it's relaxing - and talking about the game in your own time, especially with family, after a home game." — *Wendell*

Chili
(after a big game on a cold night)

1½ pounds ground beef
1 medium onion, chopped
1 can (28-ounce) crushed tomatoes
1 jar (30-ounce) spaghetti sauce
2 cans (16-ounce) kidney beans
2 to 4 tablespoons chili powder (or, to taste)

Brown beef; drain off grease. Add onion, 1 teaspoon garlic, and remaining ingredients; simmer for 15 to 20 minutes, stirring occasionally. Serve with crackers or French bread. Makes 10 servings.

* For a really hungry group, double the ingredients - and watch it disappear! Everyone will love you.
* You can freeze the remaining (if any) for a cold day.

Lemonade

12 large lemons
1 orange
sugar, very finely-granulated
ice

Wash the lemons and orange. Halve the fruit; remove the seeds. Squeeze the juice from the fruit; add the juice and squeezed fruit to a large pitcher. Chill, until serving time. Add a generous amount of ice cubes to the pitcher; stir, to dilute the lemonade. Serve with sugar on the side (so each person can sweeten his or her own). Makes 10 to 12 servings.

Drink fresh lemonade. In the hot summer days, drink plenty each day. It helps keep the body temperature down — *and, oh, those hurting cramps will be less. Outside, in the heat each day, drink it cool (not cold). Try it . . .it's good, too!*

Walls

Management and Employees
Support the
Dallas Cowboys Courage House
at
Happy Hill Farm Academy/Home

1905 North Main
Cleburne, Texas
(817) 645-0362

John & Kristine Flannery

Guard/Center

6′3″
304 lbs.

Philosophy to Live by

"Never forget where you came from." —*John*

John, Kristine, and Brennan - at her christening in 1996

Best Advice I Could Give to a High School Senior

"Don't waste your education, and pursue a higher learning." —*John*

"Finish your college education." — *Kristine*

What I Value Most

"My family." —*John and Kristine*

Biggest Challenge Ever Faced in Life

"Returning to NFL after two reconstructions on the same knee." —*John*

BORN

John - 1-13-69

Kristine - 12-14-70

COLLEGE

John - Syracuse

Kristine - Howard Brown

YEARS IN NFL

7th Year

Dallas Cowboys (2)

Houston Oilers (5)

SPOUSE'S OCCUPATION

Homemaker

ANNIVERSARY

May 1 - 4 years

CHILDREN

Brennan - 2 years

Colin Michael - newborn

PETS

4 Dogs -

(1) Labrador Retriever

and (3) Dalmatians

If I Were Not in Professional Football I Would Be

"Firefighter (ever since I was a child)." —*John*

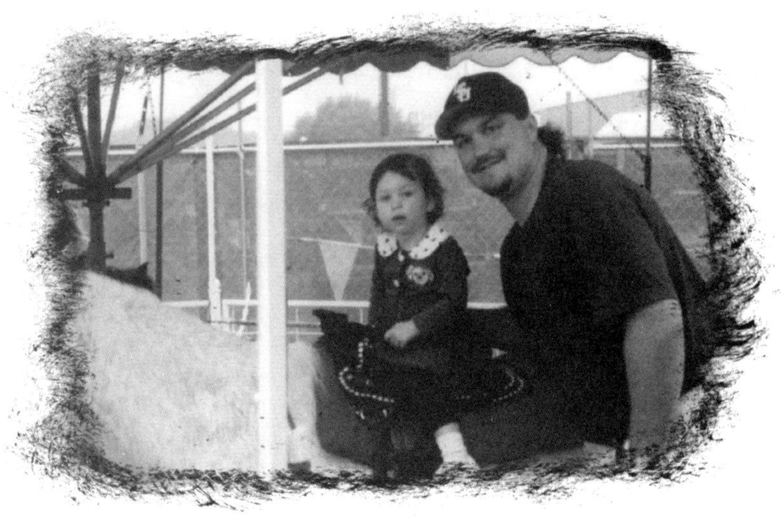

Brennan with John - at the Houston Livestock Show and Rodeo (1997)

Three People I Would Invite to a "Fantasy" Dinner Party

"JFK, Jack Ruby, and Lee Harvey Oswald *(I always have been a history buff)*." —*John*

Game Day Rituals

"Having coffee and the Sunday paper with Wade Wilson—before the wake-up call in the hotel lobby." —*John*

Favorite Pre-Game or Post-Game Meal

"Pasta and steak." —*John*

My Last Meal Would Be

"Rib-eye steak and asparagus." —*John*

"Crab claws and steak." — *Kristine*

Favorite Childhood Snack

"Pizza." —*John*

"Anything sweet." — *Kristine*

Favorite Holiday or Holiday Tradition

"July Fourth (swimming, family, and the grill)." —*John*

"Easter." — *Kristine*

Favorite City outside of Dallas

"Palm Springs, California." —*John*

"Mission Viejo, California." — *Kristine*

Hobbies and Other Interests

"Hunting, fishing, golf, and carpentry." —*John*

"Shopping." — *Kristine*

Most Memorable Moment in Life outside of Pro-Football

"Wedding day, and daughter's birth." —*John*

"Wedding day, and birth of children." — *Kristine*

Coal, pulling Brennan - in the pool (1997)

Favorite Time of Day and Why

"6:30 to 8:30 a.m. - quiet time before the family gets up (coffee, the paper, and AM News)." —*John*

"10:30 p.m. - everyone is asleep, so I have time to myself." — *Kristine*

Quiche

2 eggs, beaten
1 package hash browns
8 ounces mild Cheddar cheese
8 ounces Jalapeno cheese
½ pound cooked bacon or ham
½ cup milk

Fry hash browns enough to make workable. Put in pie plate; bake at 425 degrees for 25 minutes. Shred both cheeses; put into crust, along with bacon or ham. Over this, pour milk and eggs. Bake for 30 to 40 minutes at 350 degrees.

* You may also add mushrooms, onions, or anything you like, into the cheese mixture.

Cream Cheese Tarts

2 packages (8-ounce) cream cheese
2 eggs
¾ cup sugar
1 teaspoon vanilla
1 can fruit filling
18 vanilla wafers

Mix together cream cheese, eggs, sugar, and vanilla, until smooth. Drop a vanilla wafer into the foil liner cups in a muffin pan; fill ¾ full of mixture. Bake for 20 minutes at 350 degrees. Cool for 15 minutes; top with fruit filling.

* Keep refrigerated.

Scott Galbraith

Tight End

6′2″
255 lbs.

BORN
1-7-67

COLLEGE
USC

YEARS IN NFL
8th Year

Scott Galbraith - has returned to the Cowboys in 1997 to fill the back-up tight end position

Oven-Roasted Potatoes

2 pounds small, unpeeled, red potatoes, cut into wedges
2 to 3 tablespoons vegetable or olive oil
2 garlic cloves, minced
1 tablespoon chopped, fresh rosemary, or 1 teaspoon dried rosemary
½ teaspoon salt
¼ teaspoon pepper

Place potatoes in a 13" x 9" x 2" baking pan; drizzle oil over potatoes. Sprinkle with garlic, rosemary, salt, and pepper; toss gently (to coat). Bake at 450 degrees for 20 to 30 minutes, or until potatoes are golden brown and tender when pierced with a fork. Makes 6 to 8 servings.

Orange Carrots

1 pound carrots, peeled and sliced ¼-inch thick
½ teaspoon salt
¾ cup water
½ teaspoon grated orange peel
2 tablespoons butter, softened
1 orange, peeled, sectioned, and cut into bite-size pieces
1 tablespoon minced green onion

In a saucepan, cook carrots in salted water until crisp-tender; drain. Return carrots to pan; add orange peel, butter, orange pieces, and onion. Heat thoroughly. Serve immediately. Makes 6 servings.

Jason & Brill Garrett

Quarterback

6'2"
195 lbs.

Philosophy to Live by

"*Carpe Diem:* Seize the day." — *Jason*
"Be good to others, and
you will feel good, too." — *Brill*

Jason and Brill - at ghostly affair

BORN

Jason - 3-28-66

Brill - 12-8-65

COLLEGE

Jason - Princeton

Brill - Princeton & Harvard Law School

YEARS IN NFL

7th Year

Dallas Cowboys (6)

New Orleans Saints (1)

PETS

Maggie - Yellow Labrador Retriever

Best Advice I Could Give to a High School Senior

"Believe in yourself, work hard, and have fun." —*Jason*

"Appreciate your opportunities and your blessings. Enjoy life!" — *Brill*

What I Value Most

"Family and friends." —*Jason*

"Family, friends, and our dog." — *Brill*

Best Asset

"My husband." — *Brill*

Three People I Would Invite to a "Fantasy" Dinner Party

"Benjamin Franklin, Dr. Martin Luther King, Jr., and Albert Einstein." — *Jason*

Former Cowboys Player/Coach Most Admired and Why

"Roger Staubach - a true professional who loved to play." — *Jason*

"Roger Staubach - a terrific quarterback and respected person." — *Brill*

Garrett clan - at "Jim Garrett Day" at Susquehanna University

Game Day Rituals

"Very routine oriented - get dressed the same way, warm up the same way, etc." — *Jason*

"Via Real pre-game meal with the 'girls' and our guests, and watch pre-game warm-ups." — *Brill*

Favorite Pre-Game or Post-Game Meal

Pre-Game - "Chicken, pasta, vegetables"; and Post-Game - "Hamburger." —*Jason*

Brill & Jason - at the Tuileries Gardens in Paris, France

My Last Meal Would Be

"Turkey dinner." —*Jason*

"Stone crabs, nachos, and French fries." — *Brill*

Favorite Childhood Snack

"My mom's Oreo Cake." —*Jason*

"French fries." — *Brill*

Favorite Holiday or Holiday Tradition:

"Christmas." —*Jason and Brill*

Favorite City outside of Dallas

"New York City" —*Jason*

"New York City/Paris (tie!)." — *Brill*

Hobbies and Other Interests

"Going to movies, learning to play golf, and traveling." —*Jason*

"Traveling, going to movies, reading, relaxing by the pool, and working out." — *Brill*

Most Memorable Moment in Life outside of Pro-Football

"Wedding weekend." —*Jason and Brill*

Favorite Time of Day and Why

"Dusk - it's very peaceful." —*Jason*

"Bedtime - after a productive day." — *Brill*

Jason and Brill's Baked French Toast

1 loaf firm bread
1 package (8-ounce) cream cheese
¼ cup maple syrup
10 eggs
1½ cups half and half
8 tablespoons melted butter

Cube bread; layer half of it in a 13" x 9" pan. Cut the cream cheese into small pieces; scatter it across the bread. Cover with the remaining bread cubes. Mix eggs, half and half, syrup, and melted butter together. Pour the egg mixture over the bread in the pan. Press the bread cubes down to absorb the egg mixture. Refrigerate, in covered pan, overnight. In the morning, bake at 350 degrees for 40 to 50 minutes, until brown on top. Serve with syrup, powdered sugar, jam, or whatever you choose.

Jason and Brill *(first row, third and fourth persons on right)* - at Cousin Julie Aldridge's wedding in Chicago, Illinois

Randall Godfrey

Linebacker

6′2″
237 lbs.

Philosophy to Live by

"Winners never quit;
quitters never win." — *Randall*

BORN

4-6-73

COLLEGE

Georgia

PETS

Buddy & Killer - Miniature Doberman Pinchers

YEARS IN NFL

2nd Year

Dallas Cowboys

Randall Godfrey - only the fourth Georgia Bulldog drafted by the Cowboys - was a Consumer Economics major in college

Best Advice I Could Give to a High School Senior

"Start being responsible in order to prepare for college." — *Randall*

What I Value Most

"Waking up every morning happy." — *Randall*

Best Asset

"The way I carry myself." — *Randall*

Biggest Challenge Ever Faced in Life

"Not giving up after hurting my hamstring my senior year." — *Randall*

If I Were Not in Professional Football I Would Be

"Coaching somewhere." — *Randall*

Three People I Would Invite to a "Fantasy" Dinner Party

"Janet Jackson, Lil Kim, and my girl friend." — *Randall*

Former Cowboys Player/Coach Most Admired and Why

"Hollywood Henderson." — *Randall*

Game Day Rituals

"400 sit-ups before the game." — *Randall*

My Last Meal Would Be

"Hog chitlins." — *Randall*

Favorite Childhood Snack

"Ham and cheese sandwich." — *Randall*

Favorite Holiday or Holiday Tradition

"Christmas." — *Randall*

Favorite City outside of Dallas

"Atlanta, Georgia." — *Randall*

Hobbies and Other Interests

"Fishing, play station, and video games." — *Randall*

Most Memorable Moment in Life outside of Pro-Football

"Becoming a member of the Church of Christ." — *Randall*

Favorite Time of Day and Why

"Night time - because that's my time out." — *Randall*

Devil's Food Cake

2 sticks unsalted butter
3½ cups tightly-packed light brown sugar
3 eggs
3 squares (1 oz) unsweetened chocolate, melted and cooled
2 cups sifted cake flour
2 teaspoons baking soda
½ teaspoon salt
½ cup buttermilk
1 cup boiling water
2 teaspoons vanilla

CHOCOLATE FROSTING

2 sticks unsalted butter, softened
7 cups powdered sugar
6 squares (1-ounce) unsweetened chocolate, melted and cooled
½ cup buttermilk
¼ cup Kahlua, or other liqueur that's coffee-flavored
1 tablespoon vanilla

Preheat oven to 375 degrees. Butter and flour two 9-inch round cake pans. In a large bowl, cream together butter and brown sugar; add eggs (one at a time), beating well after each addition. Stir in the melted chocolate. In separate bowl, sift together cake flour, baking soda, and salt. Add the dry ingredients (one-third at a time) to the cake batter, alternating with the buttermilk. Pour in the boiling water and vanilla; beat, until smooth and well-mixed. Divide the batter between the prepared pans; bake for 25 to 35 minutes, or until a toothpick inserted in the center comes out clean. Remove to wire racks; let the cake layers cool completely before removing from the pans.

For the frosting: In a large bowl, cream together butter and powdered sugar. Add melted chocolate; beat, until well-blended. Slowly add buttermilk, Kahlua, and vanilla; beat, until thick and smooth. Place one cake layer on a cake plate. Spread about one-quarter of the frosting on top of the bottom layer; set the top layer in place. Frost the top and sides of the cake with the remaining frosting. Makes 1 double-layer, 9-inch round cake.

Toby Gowin

4

Punter

5'10"
167 lbs.

BORN
3-30-75

COLLEGE
North Texas

YEARS IN NFL
Rookie

Philosophy to Live by

"Be patient, and have faith." — *Toby*

Toby Gowin - an All-Big West first-team selection from the University of North Texas

Best Advice I Could Give to a High School Senior

"Find something you enjoy, and do the best you can." — *Toby*

What Do You Value Most

"My family, and the morals they taught me." — *Toby*

Best Asset

"My patience." — *Toby*

Biggest Challenge Ever Faced in Life

"Becoming a Cowboy." — *Toby*

If I Were Not in Professional Football I Would Be

"Coaching at the high school or college level." — *Toby*

Three People I Would Invite to a "Fantasy" Dinner Party

"Michael Jordan, Demi Moore, and Cindy Crawford." — *Toby*

Former Cowboys Player/Coach Most Admired and Why

"Danny White - he was a great punter." — *Toby*

Game Day Rituals

"Listen to music, and focus on game situations." — *Toby*

Favorite Pre-Game or Post-Game Meal

"Grilled chicken and pasta." — *Toby*

My Last Meal Would Be

"A nice T-bone steak and lobster." — *Toby*

Favorite Childhood Snack

"Peanut butter and jelly sandwich." — *Toby*

Favorite Holiday

"Christmas." — *Toby*

Favorite City outside of Dallas

"Austin, Texas." — *Toby*

Hobbies and Other Interests

"Golf, fishing, and hunting." — *Toby*

Favorite Time of Day and Why

"Early morning - everything is peaceful." — *Toby*

Baked Stuffed Flounder

1½ pounds shrimp, peeled and deveined
salt and pepper, to taste
cayenne pepper, to taste
2 bay leaves
3 buns
½ cup chopped celery
1 cup chopped onion
2 cloves of garlic, minced
½ cup vegetable oil
½ pound crab meat
4 eggs
½ cup cracker crumbs
¼ cup chopped green onion tops
¼ cup chopped parsley
4 medium-size flounder
butter, melted

Cook shrimp in boiling water with salt, pepper, cayenne pepper, and bay leaves for 10 minutes; drain and chop. Soak buns in 1 cup water. In a skillet, cook the celery, onion, and garlic in the oil, over medium heat, until onions are wilted. Add shrimp, crabmeat, buns, and eggs; mix well. Stir in the cracker crumbs, onion tops, and parsley; season with salt, pepper, and cayenne pepper. Split flounder lengthwise (remove backbone); stuff with shrimp mixture. Place in a baking pan; bake at 375 degrees for 45 minutes, or until fish flakes easily when tested with a fork. Brush with butter, and serve. Makes 4 servings.

Superior Squash Casserole

6 cups yellow summer squash, sliced
½ cup chopped onion
1 can (10 ¾-ounce) cream of chicken soup
1 cup sour cream
1 cup shredded carrots
1 package (8-ounce) herb-seasoned stuffing mix
½ cup butter, melted

In a saucepan, cook squash and onions in boiling salt water for 5 minutes; drain. Combine soup and sour cream together; stir in shredded carrots. Fold in squash. Combine stuffing mix and butter; spread half of stuffing mixture in the bottom of a 12" x 7" baking dish. Spoon vegetable mix on top; sprinkle remaining stuffing over vegetables. Bake at 350 degrees for 25 to 30 minutes.

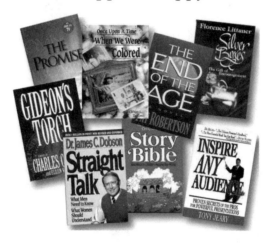

Darryl Hardy

Linebacker

6′2″
230 lbs.

BORN
11-22-68

COLLEGE
Tennessee

YEARS IN NFL
3rd Year
Dallas Cowboys(1)
Arizona Cardinals (1)
Atlanta Falcons (1)

Philosophy to Live by

"Work hard at everything you do, and good things will happen for you." — *Darryl*

Darryl Hardy - a well-rounded linebacker from the University of Tennessee

Best Advice I Could Give to a High School Senior

"Have a goal set, and go for it." — *Darryl*

What I Value Most

"The Lord allowing me to wake up everyday and enjoy my friends and family." — *Darryl*

Best Asset

"My ability to listen to people." — *Darryl*

Biggest Challenge Ever Faced in Life

"Trying to gain weight." —*Darryl*

If I Were Not in Professional Football I Would Be

"A probation officer working with young kids in trouble." —*Darryl*

Two People I Would Invite to a "Fantasy" Dinner Party

"Halle Berry and Janet Jackson." —*Darryl*

Former Cowboys Player/Coach Most Admired and Why

"Tony Dorsett - because I wanted to be a running back when I started playing football in the 5th grade." —*Darryl*

Hardy will be counted on, in 1997,
to provide depth on defense and special teams

Game Day Rituals

"Call mom for good luck." —*Darryl*

Favorite Pre-Game or Post-Game Meal

"Steak and eggs." —*Darryl*

My Last Meal Would Be

"Cheeseburger." —*Darryl*

Favorite Childhood Snack
"Baby Ruth." —*Darryl*

Favorite Holiday or Holiday Tradition
"Christmas." —*Darryl*

Favorite City outside of Dallas
"Atlanta, Georgia." —*Darryl*

Hobbies and Other Interests
"Pool, roller skating, and going to the movies." —*Darryl*

Most Memorable Moment in Life outside of Pro-Football
"Getting a scholarship to the University of Tennessee." —*Darryl*

Fantastic Burgers

- 1½ pounds ground beef
- 1 onion, chopped
- 1 tablespoon Worcestershire sauce
- 1½ teaspoons mustard
- 1 egg, beaten
- 1 cup bread crumbs, softened with water
- 1½ teaspoon salt
- ½ teaspoon pepper
- 2 tablespoons catsup
- 1 teaspoon vinegar

Mix all ingredients together well. Form into six individual patties. Grill, or broil, until done.

Crab Meat Dip

2 packages (3-ounce) cream cheese
3 tablespoons milk
1 tablespoon mayonnaise
½ cup finely-chopped celery
1 teaspoon Worcestershire sauce
2 teaspoons lemon juice
1 can (6-ounce) crab meat

In a bowl, soften cream cheese; stir in the milk and mayonnaise. Add celery, Worcestershire sauce, lemon juice, and crab meat; mix together well. Refrigerate for 1 hour before serving.

Grits Supreme Casserole

1½ cups grits
6 cups boiling water
1½ sticks butter
1 pound American cheese, grated
2 teaspoons seasoned salt
dash of Tabasco sauce
2 teaspoons salt
3 eggs, well-beaten

In a saucepan, cook grits in boiling water for 15 minutes (stir frequently). Add butter, grated cheese, seasoned salt, Tabasco sauce, salt, and beaten eggs; mix together well. Grease two casseroles; pour mixture into casseroles. Bake for 30 minutes at 350 degrees. Makes 12 servings.

George Hegamin

6′7″
331 lbs.

BORN
2-14-73

COLLEGE
North Carolina State

YEARS IN NFL
4th Year
Dallas Cowboys

George Hegamin - sampling the hors′ d′oeuvres

Marinated/Grilled Lamb Chops

- ½ cup olive oil
- ⅓ cup lime juice
- 2 teaspoons onion salt
- ½ teaspoon white pepper
- ¼ teaspoon marjoram
- ⅛ teaspoon garlic powder
- 8 lean lamb chops

Combine olive oil, lime juice, onion salt, white pepper, marjoram, and garlic powder; mix well. Pour over lamb chops; marinate in refrigerator for 8 hours, turning occasionally. Grill for 5 to 7 minutes on each side. Makes 8 servings.

Hobbies and Other Interests

"Reading, and listening to music." — *George*

Choice Apple Cake

3 eggs
2 cups granulated sugar
1 cup vegetable oil
2 cups all-purpose flour
1 teaspoon baking soda
2 teaspoons ground cinnamon
1 teaspoon vanilla
1 cup chopped walnuts
4 cups thinly-sliced tart apples

ICING:

¼ cup cream cheese, softened
4 tablespoons unsalted butter, softened
2 cups powdered sugar
1 teaspoon fresh lemon juice

Preheat oven to 350 degrees. Generously butter a 13" x 9" x 2" baking dish. In a large bowl, beat eggs with mixer, until frothy; add sugar and oil, beating until the sugar is dissolved. Mix flour, baking soda, and cinnamon together; add to the egg mixture. Add vanilla and walnuts. Spread the apples on the bottom of the baking dish; pour the batter over them. Smooth top of batter to completely cover the apples; bake for 1 hour. Set aside to cool before removing from baking dish.

For icing: After cake is cool, beat the cream cheese with the butter, until fluffy. Gradually beat in the powdered sugar and lemon juice, until well-blended and creamy.

Remove cake from baking dish; spread the icing over the top. Makes 8 servings.

Dale R. & Brooke Hellestrae

Guard/Center

6'5"
291 lbs.

Philosophy to Live by

"Do unto others as you would have them do unto you." — *Dale*

"Let your light so shine before men that they may see what you do to glorify your Father in heaven" (Matthew 5:16). — *Brooke*

The Hellestrae family - on the Boardwalk at Disney World

Best Advice I Could Give to a High School Senior

"Get your college degree; without it, you won't make a decent living." — *Dale*

"Never live or work for 'things', but concentrate on making a difference in others lives in the best way you can — lasting values!" — *Brooke*

BORN

Dale - 7-11-62

Brooke - 11-28-63

COLLEGE

Dale - SMU

Brooke - Phoenix College

YEARS IN NFL

13th Year

Dallas Cowboys (8)

Los Angeles Raiders (1)

Buffalo Bills (4)

SPOUSE'S OCCUPATION

Wife and mom

ANNIVERSARY

March 12 - 9 years

CHILDREN

Hillary - 5 years

Kendyll - 2 years

What I Value Most

"Faith, family, friends."
— Dale and Brooke

Best Asset

"Charm, wit, and good looks."
— Dale

"What Dale and I stand for together." *— Brooke*

Biggest Challenge Ever Faced in Life

"Coming back from my fractured fibula and dislocated ankle in 1989."
— Dale

"Thinking we may not experience the blessing of being parents." *— Brooke*

If I Were Not in Professional Football I Would Be

"Teacher/coach in high school." *— Dale*

The Hellestraes - at home in Scottsdale, Arizona

Three People I Would Invite to a "Fantasy" Dinner Party

(*We let Hillary and Kendyll choose*): "Jesus, Minnie Mouse, and Santa Claus [*the real one*]." *— Brooke*

Former Cowboys Player/Coach Most Admired & Why

"Billy Joe Dupree - because I played tight end growing up and wanted to play for the Cowboys." *— Dale*

Game Day Rituals

"Watching Tui go through his rituals." *— Dale*

"Having breakfast with the girls (and company that's in town) and going to the game with Tammy (Hennings)." *— Brooke*

My Last Meal Would Be

"My wife's beef stroganoff would be a hard meal to beat." —*Dale*

"A Mexican flank steak (grilled by Dale), twice-baked potatoes, cheese- broccoli casserole, a great salad, French bread, and all the hot fudge sundae I could stand - with our families." —*Brooke*

Favorite Childhood Snack

"Licking the mixing bowl beaters after my mom made frosting." —*Dale*

"Scorpa that my mom made." —*Brooke*

Kendyll and Hillary Hellestrae

Favorite Holiday or Holiday Tradition

"Watching the excitement in my children's eyes on Christmas and Easter morning." —*Dale*

"Christmas - the true meaning. Also, seeing Jason Garrett —yearly, as Santa—through our kids' eyes!" —*Brooke*

Favorite City outside of Dallas

"Maui, Hawaii." *—Dale*

"Scottsdale, Arizona." *— Brooke*

Hobbies and Other Interests

"Golf, basketball, and dominating Tui in any and all sports." *—Dale*

"I love to play most sports - racquetball would be my favorite; entertaining at our home; anything with our girls; and I've been known to play the cello and sing." *— Brooke*

Kendyll and Hillary - on Kendyll's new tricycle

Most Memorable Moment in Life outside of Pro-Football

"Birth of our girls." *—Dale*

"Our wedding day, and the day each of our girls were born." *— Brooke*

Favorite Time of Day and Why

"Sleeping in until 11:00 - because it hasn't happened since we've been parents." *—Dale*

"Watching the sunset over the desert from our deck at home in Scottsdale." *— Brooke*

Shrimp Spring Rolls

2 teaspoons dark sesame oil
1½ cups thinly-sliced green cabbage
1 cup chopped mushrooms
¾ cup chopped bean sprouts
½ cup diced carrot
⅓ cup thinly-sliced celery
¼ cup minced green onions
¼ teaspoon ground ginger
⅓ cup finely-chopped water chestnuts
2 tablespoons hoisin sauce
⅛ teaspoon pepper
2 packages (10-ounce) frozen miniature shrimp, thawed and drained
6 egg roll wrappers
1 large egg white, lightly-beaten
cooking spray

Preheat oven to 375 degrees. In a large skillet, heat oil, over medium-high heat. Add cabbage and next 6 ingredients (thru ginger); sauté for 5 minutes, or until tender - not too long! Stir in water chestnuts, hoisin sauce, pepper, and shrimp; set aside. Spoon about ¼ to ½ cup shrimp mixture into the center of each egg roll wrapper, working 1 wrapper at a time (cover remaining wrappers to keep them from drying out). Moisten edges of wrapper with a little egg white. Fold lower right corner over shrimp mixture; fold lower left and top right corners over shrimp mixture. Roll contents toward top left corner—to make a wrap. Repeat procedure with the rest of the mixture, wraps, and egg white. Place egg rolls on a baking sheet coated with cooking spray. *Lightly* coat tops of egg rolls with cooking spray. Bake at 375 degrees for 10 minutes, until *lightly browned.* Turn egg rolls over, *lightly* coat with cooking spray, and bake an additional 10 minutes, or until lightly-browned. Serve with stir-fried rice and warm plum sauce—or hot mustard, if you're brave. Serves three.

(387 calories - 6g fat - 28g protein)

Double-Chocolate Waffles

1 tablespoon butter
½ cup flour
½ cup unsweetened cocoa powder
½ cup sugar
1½ teaspoons baking powder
½ teaspoon salt
1 egg
½ cup milk
½ teaspoon vanilla
½ cup miniature chocolate chips

Heat waffle iron. Melt butter. Combine flour, cocoa, sugar, baking powder, and salt. Separate egg and yolk; beat yolk with milk and vanilla. Stir milk mixture and melted butter into flour mixture, until dry ingredients are well-moistened (batter may be slightly lumpy). Stir in chocolate chips. Beat egg white, until it holds stiff peaks; gently fold into batter. Pour batter onto waffle iron, using about ½ cup for two 4" waffles. Bake, until crisp and browned. Serve with whipped cream and raspberries or strawberries, or ice cream (my favorite!) and chocolate sauce.

Chad W., Jr. & Tammy Hennings

Defensive Tackle

6'6"
292 lbs.

Philosophy to Live by

"Love God and family, and remain committed to both." — *Chad*

Chad and Tammy, with Chase and Brenna - vacationing in Colorado (July, 1997)

Best Advice I Could Give to a High School Senior

"Experience life to the fullest, but remain true to self." — *Chad*

"Follow your conscience - always!" — *Tammy*

What I Value Most

"Family, friends, and those relationships." — *Chad and Tammy*

Best Asset

"Sincerity, and care for others." — *Chad*

"Honesty, and loyalty." — *Tammy*

BORN

Chad - 10-20-65

Tammy - 12-11-66

COLLEGE

Chad - Air Force

Tammy - Trade school

SPOUSE'S OCCUPATION

Homemaker, mom, cook, wife, etc.

CHILDREN

Chase - 4 years

Brenna - newborn

YEARS IN NFL

6th Year

Dallas Cowboys

Biggest Challenge Ever Faced in Life

"Air Force Academy, pilot training, and transition to pro-football." — *Chad*

"The illness of my son - but, praise God, He heals." — *Tammy*

If I Were Not in Professional Football I Would Be

"Rancher." — *Chad*

Three People I Would Invite to a "Fantasy" Dinner Party

"Jesus (#1), Abraham Lincoln, and John Wayne." — *Chad*

Former Cowboys Player/Coach Most Admired and Why

"Roger Staubach - similar situations." — *Chad*

"Tom Landry - just a good man!" — *Tammy*

Chad and his new girl, Brenna (July, 1997)

Game Day Rituals

"Getting the kids in order, and just getting to my seat in time for the game." — *Tammy*

Favorite Pre-Game or Post-Game Meal

"Food - lots of it!" — *Chad*

My Last Meal Would Be

"Pizza." — *Chad*

"Mexican, chocolate, and cup of coffee." — *Tammy*

Favorite Childhood Snack

"Ice cream." — *Chad*

"Oven-melted marshmallows on graham crackers." — *Tammy*

Chad and Tammy Hennings with children,
Chase and Brenna - at Fourth of July parade (1997)

Favorite Holiday or Holiday Tradition

"Christmas." — *Chad*

"Christmas Eve - listening to Christmas music, munching on good food, and anticipating Christmas morning." — *Tammy*

Favorite City outside of Dallas

"Chicago, Illinois." — *Chad*

"Cologne, Germany." — *Tammy*

Hobbies and Other Interests

"Outdoors, reading, and John Wayne movies." — *Chad*

"Golf, reading, nutrition, and being in the mountains." — *Tammy*

Most Memorable Moment in Life outside of Pro-Football

"Birth of my kids." — *Chad and Tammy*

Favorite Time of Day and Why

"Early morning - it's peaceful and quiet." — *Chad*

"Early morning - although I rarely see it." — *Tammy*

Wisconsin Cheese Soup

2 tablespoons butter
⅓ cup celery, chopped
⅓ cup onion, chopped
4 cups potatoes, diced
3 cups chicken broth
2 cups milk
parsley
salt and pepper
2 cups Cheddar cheese, shredded

Melt butter in a large saucepan. Add celery and onion; cook, until tender. Add potatoes and broth; cover, and simmer, until potatoes are tender. Stir in milk and seasonings; add cheese, until melted.
* Yummy with oyster crackers!

Honey-Lemon Chicken

4 large chicken breasts (with bone)
¼ cup honey
3 tablespoons soy sauce
1 teaspoon paprika
1 teaspoon Tabasco sauce
2 tablespoons olive oil (cold pressed)
½ cup fresh lemon juice

Remove skin from chicken breasts; arrange in baking dish. In bowl, mix honey, soy sauce, Tabasco, olive oil, and lemon juice; pour over chicken. Bake, uncovered, at 375 degrees for 1 hour.

Michael Jerome & Sandy Irvin

All-Pro
Wide Receiver

6'2"
207 lbs.

Philosophy to Live by

"Christ - the Head of our lives; He is our everything." — *Michael and Sandy*

Sandy, Michael, and Chelsea - after church (Spring, 1997)

BORN

Michael - 3-5-66

Sandy - 1-2-66

COLLEGE

Michael - Miami (FL)

Sandy - Beauty Cultural School

CHILDREN

Myesha Beyonca - 7 years

Chelsea - 2 years

Michael - newborn

YEARS IN NFL

10th Year

Dallas Cowboys

Best Advice I Could Give to a High School Senior

"Remember - every decision that you make will not only affect your life, but also the lives of the ones who love you." — *Michael*

"Continue to pursue your dreams, listen to your elders, and remember to put God first." — *Sandy*

What I Value Most

"Christ, family, and wisdom." — *Michael and Sandy*

Best Asset

"Marriage - the Divine covenant created by God." — *Michael*

"A great family." — *Sandy*

The Irvins' new blessing - Michael Jerome Irvin, II - better known as "Biscuit"

Biggest Challenge Ever Faced in Life

"Life itself." — *Michael*

If I Were Not in Professional Football I Would Be

"With the same intensity, to become a professional businessman in the world of business, in order to take care of my family." — *Michael*

Three People I Would Invite to a "Fantasy" Dinner Party

"My mother, my mother-in-law, and Jesus Himself." — *Michael*

Myesha and Chelsea - Christmas, 1996

Former Cowboys Player/Coach Most Admired and Why

"Jimmy Johnson - for his drive." — *Michael*

Game Day Rituals

"Prayer, as soon as I get on the field." — *Michael*

"Prayer for my husband." — *Sandy*

Favorite Holiday or Holiday Tradition

"Christmas." — *Michael*

Favorite City outside of Dallas

"Miami, Florida." — *Michael and Sandy*

Hobbies and Other Interests

"Video games." — *Michael*

"Shopping." — *Sandy*

Most Memorable Moment in Life outside of Pro-Football

"My children being born." — *Michael*

"Wedding day." — *Sandy*

Favorite Time of Day and Why

"Late at night - when everyone is sleeping; then, I do my thinking." — *Michael*

"Night time - after the kids are sleeping, and time with Michael." — *Sandy*

Black-Eyed Peas & Shrimp Salad

1 package (16-ounce) frozen black-eyed peas
¼ pound cooked shrimp, peeled and deveined
½ cup sliced celery
½ cup diced red bell pepper
6 green onions, sliced
¼ cup vegetable oil
2 tablespoons balsamic vinegar
1 clove garlic, minced
salt and pepper, to taste
1 small Bibb lettuce, separated into leaves

Cook peas, as directed on package; drain, and cool. In a medium bowl, gently toss peas, shrimp, celery, red bell pepper, and green onions together. Combine oil, vinegar, garlic, salt, and pepper; pour over shrimp mixture, and toss to coat. Chill. Serve on lettuce leaves. Garnish with lemon and parsley. Makes 4 servings.

Herb-Baked Catfish

2 pounds catfish fillets
2 tablespoons butter, melted
1 medium clove of garlic, minced
½ teaspoon pepper
1 teaspoon salt
¾ teaspoon paprika
½ teaspoon dried thyme
½ teaspoon dried basil
½ teaspoon dried oregano
2 tablespoons lemon juice
2 tablespoons chopped parsley

Combine garlic and melted butter; spread evenly over bottom of a 13" x 8" x 2" baking dish. Combine pepper, salt, paprika, thyme, basil, and oregano; sprinkle herb mixture on both sides of fish. Arrange fillets on top of butter mixture; drizzle with lemon juice. Bake at 350 degrees for 15 to 18 minutes, or until fish is almost done. Move the baking dish to about 4 to 6 inches from heat; broil for 4 to 6 minutes longer, or until fish flakes when tested. Remove fish to serving platter; pour pan juices over fish. Garnish with parsley. Makes 6 servings.

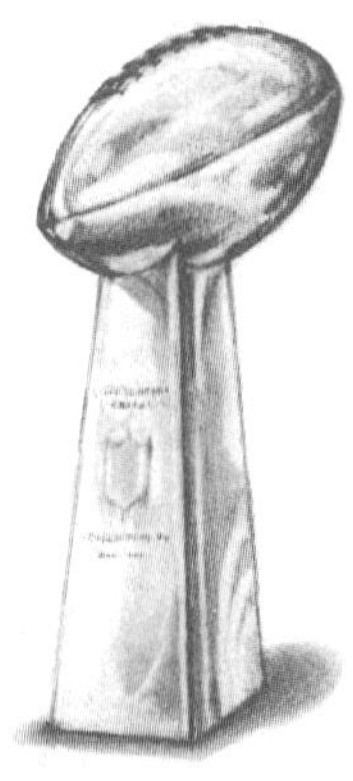

Daryl Peter "Moose" & Diane Johnston

All-Pro Fullback

6'2"
242 lbs.

Philosophy to Live by

"Start each day wanting to be better than you were the day before." — *Daryl*
"Accept responsibility for your actions." — *Diane*

Daryl and Diane Johnston - on vacation in Hawaii

BORN

Daryl - 2-10-66
Diane - 10-22-67

COLLEGE

Daryl - Syracuse

YEARS IN NFL

9th Year
Dallas Cowboys

SPOUSE'S OCCUPATION

Model

PETS

Shamus - the Golden Retriever *we don't yet own*

Best Advice I Could Give to a High School Senior

"Don't be afraid to set your goals high, because trying and not succeeding is not failing. Failure is not trying." —*Daryl*

What I Value Most

"My marriage." —*Daryl and Diane*

Mark Tuinei and Daryl - singing at a karaoke bar in Hawaii

Best Asset

"The ability to adapt to most any situation." *—Daryl*

"The drive to see things to completion." *—Diane*

Biggest Challenge Ever Faced in Life

"Staying competitive in the NFL." *—Daryl*

"Modeling in New York, and going to Spain (at the age of nineteen) alone and not being able to speak the language." *—Diane*

If I Were Not in Professional Football I Would Be

"A PGA caddie." *—Daryl*

Three People I Would Invite to a "Fantasy" Dinner Party

"Teddy Roosevelt, Franklin D. Roosevelt, and Harry Truman." *—Daryl*

Game Day Rituals

"Eat the same breakfast, arrive at the same time, and sit at Tui's locker and grade the coaches' apparel." *—Daryl*

"Talk to Daryl the first thing in the morning, work out, meet Brill Garrett, go to lunch, and on to the stadium to watch warmups." *—Diane*

Favorite Pre-Game or Post-Game Meal

"Doesn't matter, as long as I'm with friends." —*Daryl*

My Last Meal Would Be

"A big plate of hot Buffalo wings and an ice-cold beverage." —*Daryl*

"A Del Frisco's filet mignon with skillet potatoes and bread pudding for dessert." —*Diane*

Favorite Childhood Snack

"Snicker Doodle Cookies." —*Daryl*

"Peanut butter and Townhouse Crackers." —*Diane*

Favorite City outside of Dallas

"Sidney, Australia." —*Daryl*

"Quebec, Canada." —*Diane*

Hobbies and Other Interests

"Golf, drums, and reading." —*Daryl*

"Working out, cooking, reading, and learning how to use my computer." —*Diane*

Left to right: Daryl, Babe Laufenberg, Wade Wilson, Jason Garrett, Troy Aikman, and Joe Avezzano - at the Legends Car Race, benefitting the Aikman Foundation

Cornbread-Sausage Stuffing with Apples

1½ sticks butter
2½ cups finely-chopped yellow onions
3 tart apples, cored and cut into chunks
1 pound lightly-seasoned sausage
3 cups coarsely-crumbled cornbread (*homemade is best!*)
3 cups coarsely-crumbled whole wheat bread
3 cups coarsely-crumbled white bread (French)
2 teaspoons dried thyme
1 teaspoon dried sage
salt, to taste
fresh-ground black pepper, to taste
½ cup chopped Italian parsley

Melt one-half of the butter in a skillet; add onions and cook, over medium heat, until tender (25 minutes). Transfer onions and butter into a large mixing bowl. Melt remaining butter in the same skillet; add apples and cook, over high heat, until lightly-colored but not mushy. Transfer into mixing bowl with the onions. Crumble the sausage into the skillet; brown, using medium heat. Transfer into the mixing bowl, using a slotted spoon; reserve fat. Add remaining ingredients to the mixing bowl; combine gently. Cool completely before stuffing the bird. Refrigerate, if not used promptly. If you do not actually stuff the bird, spoon mixture into a casserole. Cover the casserole dish; set it in a large pan. Pour hot water around the casserole to come halfway up the sides of the dish. Bake for 30 to 45 minutes at 325 degrees, basting occasionally with juice from bird, or sausage fat, if necessary (low fat alternative is to use chicken broth instead).

* This makes enough stuffing for a 20-pound turkey, making 12 to 14 portions.

David & Melody LaFleur

Tight End

6′7″
280 lbs.

BORN

David - 1-29-74

Melody - 12-20-73

COLLEGE

David - LSU

Melody - McNeese State

YEARS IN NFL

Rookie

Best Advice I Could Give to a High School Senior

"Get an education, and never give up on your hopes and dreams." — *David*

"Never let anyone tell you what you can or cannot do, because only you know what you are capable of, and always strive to be the best at whatever you do." — *Melody*

Melody and David LaFleur

Biggest Challenge Ever Faced in Life

"Making the transition from college to the professional level." — *David*

"Moving to a different state, and leaving family and friends behind." — *Melody*

The LaFleurs - a toast to happiness

What I Value Most

"Family." —*David*

"Good health, family, and friends." —*Melody*

If I Were Not in Professional Football I Would Be

"A coach on the high school or collegiate level." —*David*

Game Day Rituals

"Trying to stay loose and relaxed." —*David*

"Tailgate parties with friends and family; and, also, prayers for David's safety, along with the rest of the players." —*Melody*

Favorite Pre-Game or Post-Game Meal

"Grilled chicken and baked potato." —*David*

My Last Meal Would Be

"Chicken and sausage gumbo." —*David*

"Roast and rice and gravy with my husband and family." —*Melody*

Favorite Childhood Snack

"Oreos and milk." —*David*

"Any kind and every kind of candy." —*Melody*

Favorite Holiday or Holiday Tradition

"Thanksgiving - the time of year, and the gathering of family." *— David*

"Christmas - getting together with family and friends." *— Melody*

Favorite City outside of Dallas

"Westlake, Louisiana - our hometown, where we met." *— David and Melody*

Hobbies and Other Interests

"Hunting and fishing." *— David*

"Reading and exercise." *— Melody*

Melody Gormanous and David LaFleur - married in May 1997

Most Memorable Moment in Life outside of Pro-Football

"My wedding day." *— David and Melody*

Favorite Time of Day and Why

"Evening - because it is a good time to slow down, relax, and enjoy one another's company." *— David and Melody*

Crawfish Fettucini

½ cup butter
2 bell peppers, diced
3 onions, diced
3 cloves garlic, diced
2 pounds crawfish tails
¼ cup flour
2 teaspoons parsley
1 pint half and half
1 pound Velveeta cheese, cubed
1 pound fettucini noodles, cooked and drained

Sauté first four ingredients; add flour. Reduce heat to low; cover. Cook for 15 minutes. Add raw crawfish and parsley; cover. Cook for 15 minutes. Add half and half, and cheese; stir well, until cheese is melted. Add cooked fettucini noodles; mix well. Put in casserole dish; bake, covered, for 15 to 20 minutes at 350 degrees. Top with Cheddar and/or Parmesan cheese (may top with bread crumbs instead of cheese).

Pralines

2 cups sugar
2 cups light brown sugar
⅔ cup white Karo syrup
⅔ cup water
3 cups pecans, chopped
¾ stick butter
2 teaspoons vanilla

Heat and boil first 4 ingredients, until thin; add pecans. Cook, medium-high heat, for approximately 30 minutes, until hard-ball stage. Turn heat off; add butter and vanilla. Stir well. Drop by spoonfuls onto wax paper.

Leon Lett

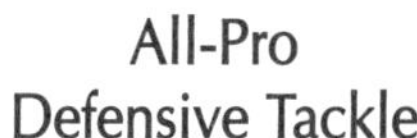

All-Pro Defensive Tackle

6'6"
295 lbs.

BORN

10-12-68

COLLEGE

Emporia State

CHILDREN

Shanavia - 10 years

YEARS IN NFL

7th Year

Dallas Cowboys

Leon Lett - nicknamed "Big Cat" by his teammates for his agility

Incomparable Bread Pudding

- 12 cups of French bread cubes, unsliced bread cut into 1-inch cubes
- 3 cups milk
- ½ cup butter, softened
- 1 cup sugar
- 4 egg yolks
- 1 teaspoon vanilla
- 1 large baking apple (peeled, cored, and thinly-cut into round slices)
- 4 egg whites
- ½ cup sugar

BOURBON SAUCE

- 1 egg, beaten
- 1 cup sugar
- ¼ cup butter
- ¾ cup whipping cream
- 2 tablespoons bourbon

Grease baking dish (8" x 8" x 2"); set aside. In large bowl, combine bread cubes and milk; let stand for 5 minutes. In another bowl, beat butter and 1 cup sugar with electric mixer, until fluffy; beat egg yolks and vanilla. Stir in bread mixture. Layer one-third bread mixture and half of apple into the baking dish; then, put one-third more bread mixture and remaining apple on top. Put remaining bread mixture on top. Place baking dish in a large baking pan; set pan on oven rack. Pour "really hot" tap water into the large baking pan to 1 inch deep. Bake in a 350 degree oven for 45 minutes, or until the center appears set.

For meringue: Beat egg whites, until they form soft peaks; add ½ cup sugar (1 tablespoon at a time), beating, on high speed, until stiff peaks form.

Remove pudding from pan of water. Spread meringue over the hot pudding, sealing meringue to the edges of dish. Return baking dish to oven; bake for 15 minutes, or till golden. Serve warm with Bourbon Sauce. Makes 8 servings.

For Bourbon Sauce: In a saucepan, combine all of the ingredients. Cook; stir, just until thickened and mixture begins to boil. Remove from heat. Carefully stir in 2 tablespoons bourbon. Slowly stir in whipping cream. Cool slightly before serving. Makes 1⅔ cups sauce.

Brock Elliott & Keri Marion

Safety

5'11"
197 lbs.

Favorite Time of Day and Why

"Morning - because it's peaceful." — *Brock*
"Early morning - my head is clear, it's quiet, and the roses look best in the light of the morning sun." — *Keri*

Marion family - at Texas Stadium (June, 1997) - Keri (holding Brock, Jr.); Brock (holding Olivia); and Briana (standing in front)

Philosophy to Live by

"Expect nothing, but prepare for everything." — *Brock*

"Always put God first . . . He will take care of the rest." — *Keri*

What I Value Most

"Family, and the Lord." — *Brock*

"My husband, and children." — *Keri*

BORN

Brock - 6-11-70

Keri - 6-5-71

COLLEGE

Brock - Nevada - Reno

Keri - Nevada - Reno & North Texas

YEARS IN NFL

5th Year

Dallas Cowboys

SPOUSE'S OCCUPATION

Homemaker

ANNIVERSARY

March 4 - 2 years

CHILDREN

Briana - 4 years

Olivia - 2 years

Brock, Jr. - 1 year

PETS

Sheba - White American Eskimo

Caesar - Tan Sharpei

Best Advice I Could Give to a High School Senior

"Take your first year of college seriously, because that sets the tempo for the rest of your college life." — *Brock*

"Do not get a credit card until after college." — *Keri*

Best Asset

"My way with my kids." — *Brock*

"My will to make things work." — *Keri*

Biggest Challenge Ever Faced in Life

"Growing up in a dysfunctional household." — *Brock*

"Going through the trials and tribulations of establishing a lifetime marriage relationship. It was worth it!" — *Keri*

Three People I Would Invite to a "Fantasy" Dinner Party

"Jesus, my Uncle David Marion (*whom I've never met*), and Grandma Clara Marion. We'd have to go to Heaven for this party!" — *Brock*

Former Cowboys Player/Coach Most Admired & Why

"Jim Jeffcoat - he was able to be a tough, hard-nosed player and a family man at the same time." — *Brock*

"As a little girl, I always liked Danny White - probably just because he was the quarterback for my favorite team." — *Keri*

Game Day Rituals

"I drink a cup of coffee and hot cocoa mixed, and get the exact same tape job every game by the same trainer, Jim Maurer." — *Brock*

"Same preparations as getting ready for any other outing, except . . . we have to be at full-speed, and there can be absolutely no stress on Dad. At least, we try!" — *Keri*

Favorite Pre-Game or Post-Game Meal

Post-Game - "A steak at Old San Francisco Steak House with some of our friends." — *Brock*

My Last Meal Would Be

"My wife's Portuguese beans with linguicia and BBQ chicken." — *Brock*

"A plate of homemade chocolate chip cookies (warm) and a tall glass of cold milk." — *Keri*

Favorite Childhood Snack

"Big bowls of Cheerios." — *Brock*

"I can't remember what I had for dinner yesterday. My favorite childhood snack. . .no clue! Maybe it was chocolate chip cookies." — *Keri*

Brock, with his two girls and their girlfriend, Jayla Allen - at the Dallas Zoo

Favorite Holiday or Holiday Tradition

"Christmas - doing the decorating and enjoying the Christmas spirit." — *Brock*

"Definitely Christmas - I start thinking about it around May of every year!" — *Keri*

Most Memorable Moment in Life outside of Pro-Football

"The day I accepted Jesus Christ as my personal Lord and Savior." — *Brock*

"My honeymoon trip to Greece. . .and walking around the Acropolis!" — *Keri*

Chocolate No-Bake Cookies

2 cups sugar
3 tablespoons cocoa
½ cup milk
1 cube butter
3 cups uncooked Quaker Quick Oats
½ cup peanut butter
1 teaspoon vanilla

Combine sugar, cocoa, milk, and butter in a saucepan. Boil for 2 minutes; remove from stove. Add oats, peanut butter, and vanilla to the boiled mixture. Stir, until all ingredients are well-blended. Drop by teaspoons onto waxed paper; let cool, until set. Store in refrigerator.

Chocolate Banana Bread

½ cup butter, softened
2 eggs
2 tablespoons cocoa
1 teaspoon salt
1 teaspoon vanilla extract
½ cup sour cream
½ cup miniature semi-sweet chocolate morsels
1 cup sugar
1½ cups flour
1 teaspoon baking soda
½ teaspoon ground cinnamon
1 cup ripe banana, mashed (approximately 3 bananas)
½ cup pecans

Cream butter; gradually add sugar. Beat, until light and fluffy. Add eggs (one at a time). In a separate small bowl, sift together dry ingredients. Add this flour mixture into the egg mixture; blend well. Add vanilla. Stir in banana, sour cream, pecans, and chocolate chips. Spoon batter into 2 greased and floured loaf pans (7½"x3"x2"). Bake at 350 degrees for 55 minutes, or until toothpick inserted in middle comes out clean. Cool for 15 minutes. Enjoy! Makes 2 loaves.

Kevin Mathis

Cornerback

5′9″
172 lbs.

BORN

4-9-74

COLLEGE

Texas A&M - Commerce

YEARS IN NFL

Rookie

Kevin Mathis - finished his senior year at Texas A&M-Commerce, leading the team with 16 punt returns for a 9.7 average and 15 kickoff returns for a 24.9 average

Ham & Potatoes au Gratin

- 2 cups sliced, peeled potatoes, cooked
- 1 cup diced, cooked ham
- 1 tablespoon minced onion
- ⅓ cup butter
- 3 tablespoons all-purpose flour
- 1½ cups milk
- 1 cup shredded Cheddar cheese
- ¾ teaspoon salt
- dash of white pepper
- chopped fresh parsley

Combine potatoes, ham, and onion in a greased casserole (1-quart); set aside. In a saucepan, melt butter, over medium heat; stir in flour, until smooth. Gradually add milk, stirring constantly, until mixture thickens and bubbles. Add cheese, salt, and pepper; stir, until the cheese melts. Pour over potato mixture; stir gently, to mix. Bake at 350 degrees for 35 to 40 minutes, or until bubbly. Garnish with parsley. Makes 2 servings.

Mexican-Style Pork Ribs

3 pounds spareribs
1 large onion, sliced
salt and pepper, to taste
1 large green pepper, chopped
½ teaspoon oregano
1 clove of garlic, minced
1 tablespoon cider vinegar
1 cup tomato sauce
1 tablespoon chili powder
1 cup hot water
½ teaspoon nutmeg
2 tablespoons flour
⅔ cup cold water

Cut the spareribs in serving pieces; in a heavy skillet, brown in a small amount of bacon drippings. Add onion; cook, until transparent. In a large casserole, place spareribs and onion; add salt and pepper, green pepper, oregano, and garlic. Mix vinegar and tomato sauce; stir in the chili powder. Pour over spareribs; add hot water. Bake for 40 minutes at 325 degrees. Mix the nutmeg, flour, and cold water; add ½ teaspoon salt. Stir into liquid in casserole; bake for 20 minutes longer. Makes 4 servings.

Hurvin McCormack

Defensive Line

6′5″
284 lbs.

BORN
4-6-72

COLLEGE
Indiana

CHILDREN
Myles - 1 year

PETS
Rah - Rottweiler

YEARS IN NFL
4th Year

Dallas Cowboys

Philosophy to Live by

"Smartest man in the world knows that he knows nothing at all." — *Hurvin*

Hurvin McCormack - has a great deal of competitiveness and desire, and is a solid contributor to the Cowboys' defensive line

Best Advice I Could Give to a High School Senior

"Absorb as much knowledge as you can." — *Hurvin*

What I Value Most

"My life, and family." — *Hurvin*

Best Asset

"Personality." — *Hurvin*

Favorite Pre-Game or Post-Game Meal

Post-Game - "Porterhouse steak." — *Hurvin*

Favorite Childhood Snack

"Pound cake." — *Hurvin*

Favorite Holiday or Holiday Tradition

"Christmas." — *Hurvin*

Favorite City outside of Dallas

"New York City." — *Hurvin*

Hobbies and Other Interests

"Golf, and listening to music." — *Hurvin*

Most Memorable Moment in Life outside of Pro-Football

"Birth of my son." — *Hurvin*

Unique Deviled Eggs

6 hard-cooked eggs, finely-chopped
1 teaspoon minced onion
3 bacon strips, fried and crumbled
½ teaspoon salt, optional
½ teaspoon pepper
¼ teaspoon prepared mustard
¼ cup mayonnaise
1 cup shredded Cheddar cheese

In a bowl, mix together eggs, onion, bacon, salt, pepper, mustard, and mayonnaise, until creamy. Form into 1-inch balls; roll in cheese. Cover, and refrigerate, until serving. Makes 25 appetizers.

Apple Cider Pound Cake

3 cups sugar
1½ cups butter
6 eggs
3 cups all-purpose flour
½ teaspoon salt
½ teaspoon baking powder
1 teaspoon ground cinnamon
½ teaspoon ground allspice
½ teaspoon ground nutmeg
¼ teaspoon ground cloves
1 cup apple cider
1 teaspoon vanilla

ICING

½ cup sugar
¼ cup butter
¼ cup buttermilk
½ teaspoon vanilla
¼ teaspoon baking soda

In a large mixing bowl, cream sugar and butter. Add eggs (one at a time), beating well after each addition. Stir together all dry ingredients; set aside. Combine cider and vanilla. Add dry ingredients, alternately with cider mixture, to batter; mix, until well-blended. Spoon into a greased 10-inch angel food cake pan, or fluted tube pan. Bake at 325 degrees for about 1 hour and 10 minutes, or until cake tests done. Meanwhile, combine all icing ingredients in a saucepan. Bring to a boil; reduce heat, and simmer for 10 minutes. While cake is warm, drizzle one-third of the icing over the cake. Serve remaining icing over individual cake servings. Makes 12 to 16 servings.

Anthony Miller

83

All-Pro
Wide Receiver

5'11"
190 lbs.

BORN
4-15-65

COLLEGE
Tennessee

CHILDREN
Two children
7 years & 2 years

YEARS IN NFL
10th Year
Dallas Cowboys (1)
Denver Broncos (3)
San Diego Chargers (6)

Best Advice I Could Give to a High School Senior

"Stay in school, and don't do drugs." — *Anthony*

Anthony Miller - provides the Cowboys with a speed receiver who has the ability to make big plays

What Do You Value Most

"My mother." — *Anthony*

Best Asset

"Running fast." — *Anthony*

Biggest Challenge Ever Face in Life

"Leaving home from high school." — *Anthony*

If I Were Not in Professional Football I Would Be

"Policeman." — *Anthony*

Three People I Would Invite to a "Fantasy" Dinner Party

"My girl (kid), mother, and grandmother." — *Anthony*

Favorite Pre-Game or Post-Game Meal

"Dinner." — *Anthony*

Favorite Childhood Snack

"Gum." — *Anthony*

Favorite Holiday or Holiday Tradition

"Fourth of July." — *Anthony*

Favorite City outside of Dallas

"San Diego, California." — *Anthony*

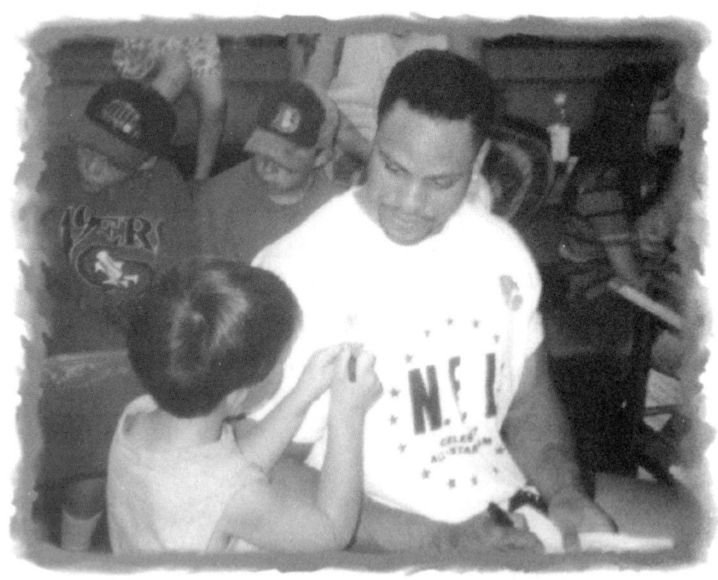

A five-time Pro-Bowl selection -
Miller joined the Cowboys on June 2, 1997

All-American Creamy Coleslaw

1 head green cabbage, coarsely-shredded
2 carrots, peeled and shredded
1 cup sour cream
½ cup mayonnaise
2 tablespoons white wine vinegar
2 tablespoons milk
1½ tablespoons sugar
2 teaspoons celery seeds
2 teaspoons freshly-ground black pepper
1 teaspoon salt
½ to 1 teaspoon Tabasco sauce

In a large bowl, toss the cabbage with the carrots. In another bowl, whisk together sour cream, mayonnaise, vinegar, milk, sugar, celery seeds, pepper, salt, and Tabasco sauce, until smooth. Pour the dressing over the slaw; toss, (to coat well). Cover, and refrigerate, until serving time. Serve cold. Makes 4 to 6 servings.

Hobbies and Other Interests

"Playing pool, and going to movies." — *Anthony*

Most Memorable Moment in Life outside of Pro-Football

"Winning the 100's and 200's in the State Meet in track." — *Anthony*

Favorite Time of Day and Why

"Night time - because I can go to sleep." — *Anthony*

Chicken and Dumplings in Herbed Broth

1 cup self-rising flour
1 teaspoon pepper
3 pounds chicken legs, thighs, and breasts
¼ cup vegetable oil
1 medium onion, chopped
2 cloves garlic, minced
1 tablespoon self-rising flour
3 cans (14½-ounce) chicken broth
2 tablespoons chopped fresh basil, or 2 teaspoons dried basil
2 tablespoons chopped fresh thyme, or 2 teaspoons dried thyme
1 tablespoon chopped rosemary, fresh or dried
½ teaspoon grated lemon rind
2 tablespoons lemon juice
2 cups self-rising flour
1 cup whipping cream
¼ cup sour cream, optional

Combine 1 cup flour and pepper; dredge chicken in flour mixture. Over medium heat, heat oil in a Dutch oven; add chicken, and cook, until golden brown. Turn once; add additional oil, if needed. Remove chicken from Dutch oven, reserving drippings in Dutch oven. Cook onion and garlic in drippings (stirring constantly), until tender. Add 1 tablespoon flour; cook 1 minute (stirring constantly); gradually add broth (stirring constantly). Add basil, thyme, rosemary, lemon rind, and lemon juice; bring to a boil. Return chicken to Dutch oven; cover, reduce heat, and simmer for 30 minutes. Remove chicken; keep warm. Reserve broth mixture in Dutch oven. Combine 2 cups self-rising flour and whipping cream, stirring with a fork (*mixture will be dry and crumbly*). Gently pat flour mixture into 2-inch balls, handling dough as little as possible. Bring reserved broth mixture to a rolling boil; add dumplings. Cover, reduce heat, and simmer (without stirring) for 7 to 10 minutes, or until dumplings are firm in the center. Remove broth mixture from heat; stir in sour cream. Serve dumplings and broth with chicken. Makes 4 servings.

Singor Mobley

Safety

5′11″
195 lbs.

BORN
10-12-72

COLLEGE
Washington State

YEARS IN NFL
Rookie

Philosophy to Live by

"Treat others the way you want to be treated." — *Singor*

Singor Mobley - safety from Washington State

Best Advice I Could Give to a High School Senior

"Work hard in school, as well as on the field."
— *Singor*

What I Value Most

"My family and friends." — *Singor*

Best Asset

"The ability to listen and learn from what I hear." — *Singor*

Biggest Challenge Ever Faced in Life

"The death of my grandmother and grandfather - in my rookie season in the CFL." — *Singor*

If I Were Not in Professional Football I Would Be

"A firefighter." — *Singor*

Two People I Would Invite to a "Fantasy" Dinner Party

"Malcolm X, and my girl friend's father (he passed away before I met him)." — *Singor*

Former Cowboys Player/Coach Most Admired & Why

"Tony Dorsett - because of the positive way he portrayed NFL football." — *Singor*

Game Day Rituals

"Clean my shoes, and listen to "DCP". — *Singor*

Favorite Pre-Game or Post-Game Meal

Pre-Game - "Pancakes." — *Singor*

My Last Meal Would Be

"Chicken Fettucini Alfredo." — *Singor*

Favorite Childhood Snack

"Peanut butter and jelly." — *Singor*

Favorite Holiday or Holiday Tradition

"Thanksgiving." — *Singor*

Favorite City outside of Dallas

"Seattle, Washington." — *Singor*

Hobbies and Other Interests

"Snowboarding, Sony play station, and golf." — *Singor*

Most Memorable Moment in Life outside of Pro-Football

"The birth of my little brother." — *Singor*

Favorite Time of Day and Why

"Night - because the stars and moon are out." — *Singor*

Singor's Dishwasher Salmon

1 teaspoon olive oil
2 salmon filets (6 ounces each)
juice of 1 lemon
salt
pepper
fresh dill

Drizzle a teaspoon of olive oil on a 14" x 14" piece of heavy-duty foil. Add the juice of one lemon, salt, pepper, and some fresh dill. Wrap the foil around the fish; create an airtight seal by folding the edges over several times and pinching tightly. Place the package on the top rack of your dishwasher and run it through the entire wash and dry cycle. Use high-heat setting (*don't try to do a load of dishes at the same time*).

Banana Bread

1¾ cups all-purpose flour
⅔ cup sugar
2 teaspoons baking powder
½ teaspoon baking soda
¼ teaspoon salt
1 cup mashed, ripe bananas
⅓ cup shortening or margarine
2 tablespoons milk
2 eggs
¼ cup chopped nuts (optional)
¼ teaspoon vanilla extract

In a large mixer bowl, combine 1 cup of the flour, sugar, baking powder, baking soda, and salt. Add mashed bananas, shortening or margarine, and milk. Beat with an electric mixer, on low speed, until blended; then, beat, on high speed, for 2 minutes. Add eggs and vanilla extract; then, add remaining flour. Beat, until well-blended. Stir in nuts. Pour batter into a greased 8" x 4" x 2" loaf pan. Bake in a 350 degree oven for 55 to 60 minutes, or until a toothpick inserted in the center comes out clean. Cool for 10 minutes on a wire rack. Remove from pan; cool thoroughly on a wire rack.

Nathaniel "Nate", Jr. & Dorothy Newton

All-Pro Guard

6′3″
320 lbs.

Philosophy to Live by

"Be your own man." — *Nate*
"Always ask yourself: 'Is this something that God would do' - before making decisions." — *Dorothy*

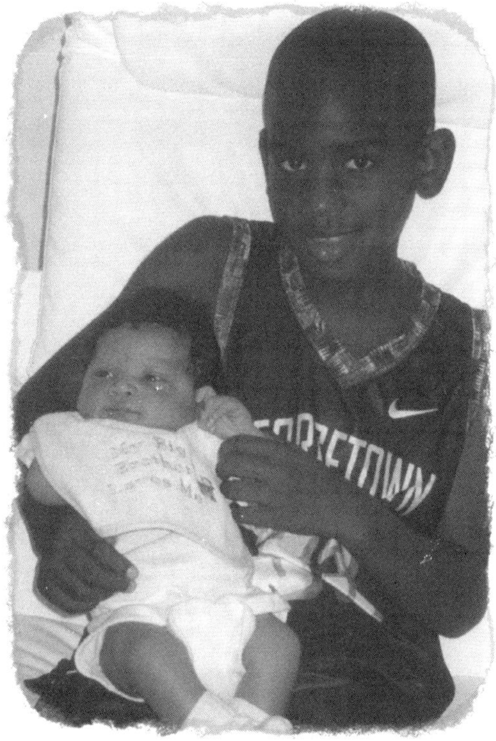

Nathaniel Newton, III "Tre" - 7 years; and Nate "King" Newton - 4 weeks

Best Advice I Could Give to a High School Senior

"Make your own decision." — *Nate*
"Make the most of every opportunity." — *Dorothy*

BORN

Nate - 12-20-61

Dorothy - 12-20-61

COLLEGE

Nate - Florida A & M

Dorothy - Southwestern Louisiana - Lafayette

YEARS IN NFL

12th Year

Dallas Cowboys

SPOUSE'S OCCUPATION

Husband's local agent/secretary

ANNIVERSARY

January 30

CHILDREN

Nathaniel, III - "Tre" - 7 years

Nate "King" - newborn

What I Value Most

"The Inner Spirit - God being the Inner Spirit." — *Nate*

"Allowing Christ to live in me" (Galatians 2:20). — *Dorothy*

Best Asset

"My wife." — *Nate*

"Nathaniel Newton, III, and Nate King Newton." — *Dorothy*

Biggest Challenge Ever Faced in Life

"Trying to keep my family together." — *Nate*

"Maintaining a Christian-based environment." — *Dorothy*

If I Were Not in Professional Football I Would Be

"Working an honest 9-5 job." — *Nate*

Three People I Would Invite to a "Fantasy" Dinner Party

"Muhammad Ali, Malcolm X, and my dad - Nathaniel Newton, Sr." — *Nate*

Former Cowboys Player/Coach Most Admired and Why

"Tony Dorsett - always showed up for big games; and Jimmy Johnson - he believed in me." — *Nate*

"Kelvin Martin - player; and Jimmy Johnson - coach." — *Dorothy*

Game Day Rituals

"Come home before game to see my family." — *Nate*

"Turn off phones, lock doors, close private gate, and visit with Nate quietly (hardly any talking)." — *Dorothy*

Favorite Pre-Game or Post-Game Meal

"Pasta, chicken, rice, and baked potato." — *Nate*

Favorite Childhood Snack

"McDonald's French fries." — *Nate*

"Cereal." — *Dorothy*

Hobbies and Other Interests

"Raising American Pit Bull Terriers." — *Nate*

"Supporting our son's during daily activities; and competitive volleyball, softball, and basketball." — *Dorothy*

Most Memorable Moment in Life outside of Pro-Football

"Watching my first son born - Nathaniel Newton, III (Tre)." — *Nate*

"The birth of both of our sons." — *Dorothy*

Favorite Time of Day and Why

"5:30 p.m. - sitting around the house." — *Nate*

"All day - because it involves our kids, and then, by 8:00 p.m., the kids are taken care of and we have finished dinner; then, it's my time to spend with my husband or do whatever I want." — *Dorothy*

Barbecued Spareribs

- 1 fresh onion, chopped
- 2 tablespoons brown sugar
- 1 teaspoon paprika
- 1 teaspoon salt
- 1 teaspoon dry mustard
- 1 teaspoon chili powder
- 2 dashes of Tabasco sauce
- 3 tablespoons Worcestershire sauce
- ¼ cup vinegar
- 1 cup tomato juice
- ¼ cup catsup
- ½ cup water
- 3 pounds spareribs
- 1 fresh lemon, thinly-sliced

Mix the onion, brown sugar, paprika, salt, mustard, chili powder, Tabasco, Worcestershire sauce, vinegar, tomato juice, catsup, and water in a saucepan; simmer for 15 to 20 minutes. Cover; set aside. Cut spareribs into serving pieces; place on rack in a shallow baking pan. Place a lemon slice on each serving piece. Bake at 450 degrees for 30 minutes. Pour the sauce over the spareribs. Reduce temperature to 350 degrees; cover, and bake for 1 hour and 30 minutes more (baste frequently). Makes 6 servings.

Old-Fashioned Peach Cobbler

FILLING

12 fresh peaches (may substitute frozen)
1 stick butter
1½ tablespoons flour
1 cup sugar
⅛ teaspoon nutmeg
¼ teaspoon ground cloves
juice of ½ lemon

PASTRY

1 cup flour
2 tablespoons sugar
¼ teaspoon salt
⅛ teaspoon nutmeg
4 tablespoons shortening
4 tablespoons ice water

For the filling: Peel peaches; dice into ¼" cubes. Melt butter. Add flour; stir, until smooth. Add sugar, nutmeg, cloves, lemon juice, and peaches. Mix well; set aside.

To make the pastry: Mix flour, sugar, salt, and nutmeg together; add shortening. Mix, until it has a coarse texture. Add ice water; stir with spoon (*use as few strokes as possible*). Roll out dough on floured surface. Prepare 4 pastry shells to fit any deep-sided baking dish (9" x 5", or 8" square). Bake two of the shells at 350 degrees, until golden brown; cool.

Place 1 unbaked shell in bottom of dish. Add layer of peach filling. Place baked shell on top of the peaches; top with more filling. Add a second baked shell; cover with remaining peach filling. Top with final unbaked pastry (to cover the dish). Bake at 350 degrees for 45 minutes, or until golden brown. Makes 8 servings.

Kavika Pittman

97

Defensive End

Best Advice I Could Give to a High School Senior

"Get your education - because it's hard in this world." — *Kavika*

6'6"
270 lbs.

BORN

2-9-74

COLLEGE

McNeese State

YEARS IN NFL

2nd Year
Dallas Cowboys

Kavika Pittman - the first McNeese State University player ever drafted by the Cowboys

What I Value Most

"My life." — *Kavika*

Best Asset

"My loving family - they've always been supportive of me and the things I've done." — *Kavika*

Biggest Challenge Ever Faced in Life

"Playing pro football." — *Kavika*

If I Were Not in Professional Football I Would Be

"I think that I would be coaching football somewhere." — *Kavika*

My Last Meal Would Be

"Smothered pork chop, mashed potatoes with brown gravy, and green beans." — *Kavika*

Favorite Childhood Snack

"Little Debbie cakes." — *Kavika*

Pittman - a Health and Human Performance major in college

Favorite City outside of Dallas

"Atlanta, Georgia." — *Kavika*

Hobbies and Other Interests

"Video games." — *Kavika*

Favorite Time of Day and Why

"Night - because of the night life." — *Kavika*

Rhubarb Pie

PASTRY:

2¼ cups sifted all-purpose flour
2 teaspoons salt
¼ cup vegetable shortening
sugar (for sprinkling)

FILLING:

3 cups diced, fresh spring rhubarb
1½ cups sugar
¼ cup all-purpose flour

Preheat oven to 425 degrees. For pastry: In a large bowl, combine flour and salt. Remove ⅓ cup of the mixture, and place in a small bowl; set the large bowl aside. Add ½ cup cold water to the small bowl; stir well (to make a paste). Set aside. To large bowl, add shortening; cut it into the flour, using a pastry blender or two knives, until the mixture is like a coarse meal. Add the paste; stir with a fork, until the dough pulls together enough to form a ball. Divide the dough in half. Wrap one half in a plastic wrap; refrigerate. On a lightly-floured surface, roll out the other half of dough to about ⅛-inch thickness. Place the dough into a pie pan (9-inch); set aside. For filling: In a bowl, combine the rhubarb, sugar, and flour; toss well to coat the rhubarb with the sugar and flour. Turn the rhubarb into the pie crust. Roll out remaining dough; place over the rhubarb filling. Trim the edges and crimp them. Cut 5 small slits in the top crust (to allow steam to escape). Sprinkle top of the pie with sugar. Place the pie on a baking sheet; bake for 20 minutes. Lower the oven temperature to 350 degrees; bake for 25 minutes more, or until the crust is golden brown. Serve warm, or at room temperature. Makes 6 to 8 servings.

Deion Luwynn Sanders

All-Pro Cornerback

6'1"
195 lbs.

Other NFL teams often simply refuse to throw the football Deion's way, because of his ability to take half of the field away from opposing offenses

BORN

8-9-65

COLLEGE

Florida State

CHILDREN

Deiondra - 7 years

Deion Luwynn, Jr. - 4 years

YEARS IN NFL

9th Year

Dallas Cowboys (3)

San Francisco 49ers (1)

Atlanta Falcons (5)

Hobbies and Other Interests

"Fishing." —*Deion*

Salmon Croquettes

1 can (1-pound) sock-eye salmon, drained
½ teaspoon salt
dash of cayenne pepper
1 tablespoon chopped parsley
¼ cup cracker crumbs
½ teaspoon grated onion
1 egg, beaten
1 cup bread crumbs
1 egg beaten

Finely mince fish; add salt, pepper, parsley, cracker crumbs, onion, and egg. Mix well. Roll into patties; dip these into beaten egg, and roll in bread crumbs. Drop into deep hot fat and fry, until light brown; drain on paper towels. Serve immediately with tartar sauce, or red sauce. Makes 4 servings.

Deion Sanders - a gifted and versatile athlete - is also a major league baseball player

Chicken Fajita Salad

2 tablespoons cooking oil, divided
¼ cup lime juice
1 garlic clove, minced
½ teaspoon ground cumin
½ teaspoon oregano
1 pound chicken breasts (boneless, skinless), cut into thin strips
1 onion, cut into thin wedges
1 sweet red pepper, cut into thin strips
1 can (7-ounce) chopped green chilies, drained
1 cup whole almonds, toasted
shredded lettuce
3 tomatoes, cut into wedges
1 avocado, sliced

Combine 1 tablespoon oil, lime juice, garlic, cumin, and oregano; toss with chicken. Marinate for at least 30 minutes. Meanwhile, in a skillet, heat remaining oil, on medium-high; sauté onion for 2 minutes. Drain chicken, reserving marinade. Add chicken to skillet; stir-fry, until it begins to brown. Add red pepper, chilies, and marinade; cook for 2 minutes. Stir in almonds. Serve immediately over shredded lettuce; top with tomatoes and avocado. Makes 4 to 6 servings.

Steve Scifres & Amanda Collins

Tackle/Guard

6′4″
300 lbs.

BORN

Steve - 1-22-72

Amanda (fiancee) - 11-18-76

COLLEGE

Steve - Wyoming

YEARS IN NFL

Rookie

Best Advice I Could Give to a High School Senior

"There is no such thing as a free lunch." — *Steve*

"Don't be stereotyped by society." — *Amanda*

Steve Scifres with fiancee, Amanda Collins - to be married February 14, 1998

Philosophy to Live by

"The most important thing in life is a personal relationship with Jesus." — *Steve*

"Go with God." — *Amanda*

What I Value Most

"My relationship with Jesus, and my relationship with family." — *Steve*

"Love." — *Amanda*

If I Were Not in Professional Football I Would Be

"Working with children." — *Steve*

Three People I Would Invite to a "Fantasy" Dinner Party

"Amy Grant, Brennan Manning, and William Wallace." — *Steve*

Game Day Rituals

"Think quietly about the game, listen to music, and pray." — *Steve*

"Pray." — *Amanda*

Steve - with dad (Jim); mom (Rosemarie); and brother (James) and his wife (Norma)

Favorite Pre-Game or Post-Game Meal

"Italian." — *Steve*

My Last Meal Would Be

"Veal Saltimboca and Fettucini Alfredo." — *Steve*

"Macaroni and cheese." — *Amanda*

Favorite Childhood Snack

"Reese's Peanut Butter Cups." — *Steve*

"Fruit roll-ups." — *Amanda*

Favorite Holiday or Holiday Tradition

"Easter." — *Steve*

"Christmas." — *Amanda*

Favorite City outside of Dallas

"Colorado Springs, Colorado." — *Steve*

"Ft. Collins, Colorado." — *Amanda*

Hobbies and Other Interests

"Skiing, rock climbing, cooking, and country swing." — *Steve*

"Waterskiing, playing the piano, gymnastics, roller blading, singing, and country swing." — *Amanda*

Chicken Marsala

2 pounds boneless, skinless chicken breasts
flour
salt and pepper
olive oil
1 can beef bouillon or consommé
1 cup marsala wine

Slice or pound chicken breasts very thin. Dredge chicken in flour, seasoned with salt and pepper; sauté, in 2 tablespoons olive oil, until browned, adding oil as needed. Remove chicken to a platter. Add one-half can of bouillon, or consommé, and ½ cup marsala to pan. Return chicken to pan; cover, and simmer for 10 to 15 minutes (turning once). Remove chicken to platter; keep warm. Add remaining soup and marsala to pan, simmering until reduced by half. Pour over chicken; serve. Makes 4 to 6 servings.

* Serve with mashed potatoes, or buttered noodles, and steamed green beans, seasoned with garlic powder.

Caesar Salad

1 large head romaine lettuce, washed and dried
⅔ cup olive oil
2 eggs
1 or 2 tablespoons lemon juice
1½ tablespoons garlic powder
5 or 6 drops Worcestershire sauce
1 teaspoon Coleman's mustard
½ cup grated Parmesan cheese
croutons, to taste
3 or 4 twists freshly-ground black pepper

Wrap cleaned lettuce in towel; chill. Coddle eggs in very hot water for about 10 minutes. Using a wire whisk, beat eggs in deep bowl or measuring bowl; add olive oil, and whisk, until thickened. Add lemon juice, garlic powder, Worcestershire sauce, mustard, pepper; whisk thoroughly. Put chilled lettuce in a large bowl; add croutons, to taste. Add Parmesan cheese to dressing; whisk, until mixed. Pour dressing over lettuce; mix and serve. Makes 4 to 6 servings.

* Can be used as a main dish by adding grilled, boneless chicken breast.

Most Memorable Moment in Life outside of Pro-Football

"Different special times with family." — *Steve*

"Getting engaged." — *Amanda*

Favorite Time of Day and Why

"Sunset - it's peaceful, spectacular, and relaxing." — *Steve*

"Morning - because God's creation seems most beautiful." — *Amanda*

Clay Shiver

50

Philosophy to Live by

"To love God with all of your heart, soul, mind, and strength." — *Clay*

Center

6′2″
294 lbs.

BORN
12-7-72

COLLEGE
Florida State

YEARS IN NFL
2nd Year
Dallas Cowboys

Clay Shiver - only the fifth starting center in the previous 22 seasons for the Dallas Cowboys

Best Advice I Could Give to a High School Senior

"Hard work and education will go a long way toward your dreams." — *Clay*

What I Value Most

"My faith, and my family." — *Clay*

Biggest Challenge Ever Faced in Life

"Professional football." — *Clay*

If I Were Not in Professional Football I Would Be

"In coaching, or a mechanic." — *Clay*

Former Cowboys Player/Coach Most Admired and Why

"Ray Donaldson." — *Clay*

Game Day Rituals

"Coffee and reading." — *Clay*

Favorite Pre-Game or Post-Game Meal

"Chicken and pasta." — *Clay*

My Last Meal Would Be

"Anything my mom cooks." — *Clay*

Clay - the top center in the '96 draft - has the intelligence, toughness, and ability to be an outstanding center for the Cowboys

Shriver - a Business major at Florida State University

Favorite Childhood Snack

"Pizza." — *Clay*

Favorite City outside of Dallas

"Tallahassee, Florida." — *Clay*

Hobbies and Other Interests

"Movies, reading, and computers." — *Clay*

Most Memorable Moment in Life outside of Pro-Football

"Anytime my family has all been together." — *Clay*

Favorite Time of Day and Why

"Supper time." — *Clay*

Shrimp Dip

2 packages (8-ounce) cream cheese
½ cup mayonnaise
1 clove garlic, crushed
2 teaspoons grated onion
2 teaspoons prepared mustard
2 teaspoons sugar
dash of salt
2 cups shrimp, cut up
6 tablespoons sauterne

Melt cheese, over low heat. While stirring, blend in mayonnaise, garlic, onion, mustard, sugar, and salt. Stir in shrimp and wine; heat thoroughly. Pour in chafing dish. Serve hot with Triscuits.

* This dip can be made ahead, but add wine right before serving.

Spinach Casserole

½ pound sliced bacon
2 packages frozen chopped spinach
2 eggs
2 cups milk
1 teaspoon salt
⅔ cup soft bread crumbs
1½ cups shredded Provolone cheese
paprika

Dice bacon, and pan broil, until crisp; drain on paper towels. Cook spinach, according to directions; drain thoroughly. Beat eggs slightly; add milk and salt. Stir in the spinach, bread crumbs, bacon, and half of the cheese; pour mixture into baking dish (1½-quart). Sprinkle remaining cheese around the outside edge; sprinkle with paprika. Bake at 375 degrees for 30 to 35 minutes. Makes 8 servings.

Emmitt J. Smith, III

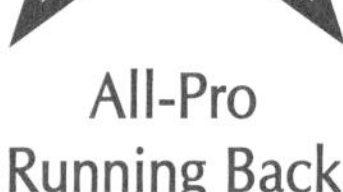

All-Pro
Running Back

5′9″
209 lbs.

BORN
5-15-69

COLLEGE
Florida

YEARS IN NFL
8th Year
Dallas Cowboys

Best Advice I Could Give to a High School Senior

"Try to get a higher education." — *Emmitt*

Emmitt Smith - one of the all-time great running backs in NFL history

What I Value Most

"My relationship with Christ, and my family."
— *Emmitt*

Biggest Challenge Ever Faced in Life

"Leaving high school and home to go to college." — *Emmitt*

If I Were Not in Professional Football I Would Be

"State trooper." — *Emmitt*

© James D. Smith Photography

Emmitt is the only non-kicker to accomplish three career 100-point seasons in Dallas' history

My Last Meal Would Be

"Breakfast." —*Emmitt*

Favorite Childhood Snack

"Fireballs." —*Emmitt*

Favorite Holiday or Holiday Tradition

"Christmas." —*Emmitt*

Favorite City outside of Dallas

"Atlanta, Georgia." —*Emmitt*

Hobbies and Other Interests

"Golf, and movies." —*Emmitt*

Most Memorable Moment in Life outside of Pro-Football

"College graduation." —*Emmitt*

Amaretto Cheesecake

15 chocolate sandwich cookies with white filling, broken up
1 cup blanched whole almonds
⅓ cup sugar
¼ cup butter, softened
3 packages (8-ounce) cream cheese, softened
1 cup sugar
4 eggs
½ cup amaretto
⅓ cup whipping cream
1 teaspoon vanilla
¼ cup toasted, sliced almonds

For crust:

In a food processor bowl, place cookies, blanched whole animals, ⅓ cup sugar, and butter; cover, and process, until mixture is like fine crumbs. Press mixture on the bottom and about 1½ to 2 inches up the sides of a 9-inch springform pan; set aside.

For filling:

In a large bowl, beat cream cheese and 1 cup sugar with electric mixer, until smooth; add eggs. Beat, on low speed, just until combined; stir in amaretto, whipping cream, and 1 teaspoon vanilla. Pour filling into the crust-lined springform pan.

Carefully place cheesecake on a shallow baking pan; bake at 375 degrees for 40 minutes. Stir together sour cream, 1 tablespoon sugar, and 1 teaspoon vanilla; carefully spread this mixture on top of the cheesecake. Return cheesecake to oven; bake at 375 degrees for 5 minutes more.

Cool in pan for 15 minutes; loosen crust from the sides of the pan. Cool for 30 minutes more; remove sides of the pan. Cool for 4 hours; cover, and refrigerate, until serving time. Garnish with toasted, sliced almonds. Makes 12 servings.

Kevin Rey Smith

Cornerback

5′11″
190 lbs.

BORN
4-7-70

COLLEGE
Texas A&M

YEARS IN NFL
6th Year
Dallas Cowboys

CHILDREN
Kevaughn Rae - 4 years

PETS
Bailey and Mikie - Dogs

Best Advice I Could Give to a High School Senior

"Prepare yourself to make decisions." — *Kevin*

© James D. Smith Photography

Kevin Smith - Ed Block Courage Award recipient - for his triumphant and courageous return to the lineup, after suffering a ruptured right Achilles tendon, in 1995

Philosophy to Live by

"Never live through expectations - expectations usually lead to disappointment." — *Kevin*

What I Value Most

"Christ, and my family - I try hard not to value material things." — *Kevin*

Best Asset

"Sense of humor." — *Kevin*

Biggest Challenge Ever Faced in Life
"Recovering from an Achilles tendon tear." — *Kevin*

If I Were Not in Professional Football I Would Be
"More than likely, coaching." — *Kevin*

Favorite Pre-Game or Post-Game Meal
"Pasta." — *Kevin*

My Last Meal Would Be
"Seafood." — *Kevin*

Favorite Childhood Snack
"Any kind of fruit, except watermelon." — *Kevin*

Favorite City outside of Dallas
"Houston, Texas." — *Kevin*

Kevin has 15 career interceptions - more than any current Cowboys player has collected while wearing a Dallas' uniform

Hobbies and Other Interests

"Fishing, collecting C.D.'s, and reading." — *Kevin*

Most Memorable Moment in Life outside of Pro Football

"Having Kevaughn." — *Kevin*

Favorite Time of Day and Why

"Night - I usually fall asleep late (somewhere between 10:00 p.m. and 1:30 a.m.) - I read and listen to music." — *Kevin*

Shrimp Etouffee

1 pound peeled shrimp
½ cup butter
½ cup onion, coarsely-chopped
½ cup celery, coarsely-chopped
1 cup bell pepper, coarsely-chopped
2 cups sliced mushrooms
2 tablespoons chopped parsley
2 cloves garlic, minced
½ cup water
1 tablespoon flour
⅓ cup dry sherry wine
juice of ½ lemon
¼ teaspoon salt
¼ teaspoon white pepper
1 cup green onions, coarsely-chopped

Melt butter; quickly stir-fry all vegetables together. Cook, over medium heat, for 5 minutes, stirring constantly. Gradually add the water, flour, and wine, stirring constantly. Add shrimp, lemon juice, salt, and pepper. Stir, cover, and simmer for 8 to 10 minutes. Serve over hot rice. Makes 4 servings.

Savory Crab Cakes

1 pound fresh lump crab meat (remove shell pieces)
1⅓ cups soft bread crumbs
⅓ cup minced green onions
⅓ cup chopped, fresh parsley
2 tablespoons lemon juice
1 tablespoon milk
1 teaspoon hot sauce
½ teaspoon salt
¼ teaspoon pepper
4 egg whites, lightly-beaten
1⅓ cups soft bread crumbs
2 tablespoons vegetable oil, divided
lemon wedges

Combine first 10 ingredients in a bowl; stir well. Shape mixture into 8 patties (½-inch thick). Place 1⅓ cups soft bread crumbs in a shallow dish; coat patties with bread crumbs. In a large non-stick skillet, heat 1 tablespoon vegetable oil, over medium-high heat. Add 4 coated patties; cook for 3 minutes. Carefully turn patties; cook for 3 minutes, or until patties are golden brown. Repeat procedure with remaining 1 tablespoon vegetable oil and remaining 4 coated patties. Serve crab cakes with lemon wedges. Makes 8 crab cakes.

Vinson & Anne Smith

Linebacker

6′2″
248 lbs.

BORN

Vinson - 7-3-65

COLLEGE

Vinson - East Carolina

Anne - Howard University & Virginia

YEARS IN NFL

10th Year

SPOUSE'S OCCUPATION

Mother & business manager for their real estate company

ANNIVERSARY

May 14 - 2 years

CHILDREN

Payton - 1 year

Jayme - 12 years

Philosophy to Live by

"Be kindhearted, forgiving, and loving." — *Anne*

Vinson Smith - with daughter, Payton

What I Value Most

"My relationship with God, my family and friends, and my health." — *Anne*

Biggest Challenge Ever Faced in Life

"Raising a child." — *Anne*

If I Were Not in Professional Football I Would Be

"Lawyer/teacher." — *Vinson*

Three People I Would Invite to a "Fantasy" Dinner Party

"Tony Tolbert, Will Downing, and Vic Wilkins." — *Vinson*

Payton Smith - 16 months

Former Cowboys Player/Coach Most Admired and Why

"Dave Wannstedt." — *Vinson*

Game Day Rituals

"Attend early morning church service, and watch cartoons with Payton, while she eats breakfast." — *Anne*

My Last Meal Would Be

"Spaghetti." — *Vinson*

Favorite Childhood Snack

"Potato chips." — *Vinson*

"Raisins, and popcorn." — *Anne*

Favorite Holiday or Holiday Tradition

"Christmas." — *Vinson*

"A Christmas village - filled with little houses, trees, people, horse-drawn carriages, etc. - and assembling the train around a 7' Douglas Fir from North Carolina." — *Anne*

Favorite City outside of Dallas

"Chicago, Illinois." — *Vinson*

"London, England." — *Anne*

Hobbies and Other Interests

"I enjoy volunteering at hospitals and other social service agencies. I also enjoy playing the piano and writing." — *Anne*

Favorite Time of Day and Why

"Early morning - it's cool and peaceful, and a quiet time to think and plan my day." — *Anne*

Star Cheese Bites

½ cup butter
2 cups shredded, extra-sharp Cheddar cheese
2½ cups all-purpose flour
¾ teaspoon salt
¾ teaspoon ground red pepper
⅓ cup cold water

Beat butter, at medium speed, with electric mixer; add cheese, beating, until blended. Combine flour, salt, and red pepper; gradually add to cheese mixture, beating, until blended, after each addition. Add water, beating, until mixture forms a firm dough. Roll dough to ½-inch thickness on a lightly-floured surface. Cut, using a 1½-inch star-shaped cutter; place on lightly-greased baking sheets. Bake at 350 degrees for 15 minutes, or until golden. Remove from pans; cool on wire racks. Store in an air-tight container. Makes 4½ dozen.

Chicken & Asparagus Casserole

12 chicken breast halves, boneless
1 medium onion, chopped
1 stick butter
1 can (8-ounce) button mushrooms, drained
1 can (10½-ounce) cream of chicken soup
1 can (5½-ounce) evaporated milk
½ pound sharp Cheddar cheese, grated
Tabasco sauce, to taste
2 teaspoons soy sauce
1 teaspoon salt
1 jar (4-ounce) pimentos, drained and chopped
2 packages (10-ounce) frozen asparagus spears
½ cup slivered almonds

Cook chicken in seasoned water, until done; cut into bite-size pieces, and set aside. Sauté onion in butter, until limp; add remaining ingredients (except asparagus and almonds). Cook asparagus, according to directions on package; drain well. When cheese has melted in the sauce, begin to layer ingredients in a casserole (3-quart): layer of chicken, layer of asparagus, and layer of cheese sauce. Repeat layers. Top with almonds. Bake at 350 degrees, until bubbly.

Vinson's wife, Anne, and daughter, Payton

Omar Stoutmire

Safety

5′11″
198 lbs.

BORN
7-9-74

COLLEGE
Frenso State

YEARS IN NFL
Rookie

Omar Stoutmire - the first Fresno State defensive player ever drafted by Dallas

Chocolate-Blueberry Squares

- 1 package (8½-ounce) chocolate wafer cookies, crushed (about 2 cups)
- ½ cup butter, melted
- 2 egg whites
- 2 cups sifted powdered sugar
- 1 package (8-ounce) cream cheese, softened
- 1 can (21-ounce) blueberry pie filling
- 1 cup chopped pecans, divided
- 1½ cups whipping cream
- 3 tablespoons sugar
- ½ teaspoon vanilla
- ½ cup semi-sweet chocolate morsels
- 2 tablespoons milk

Combine cookie crumbs and butter, stirring well. Press mixture into the bottom of an ungreased 9-inch square pan. Bake at 350 degrees for 10 minutes. Beat egg whites (at room temperature), until foamy; gradually add powdered sugar, beating until blended. Add cream cheese; beat, until smooth. Spread mixture evenly over the crust; top with pie filling, and sprinkle with ¾ cup pecans. Beat whipping cream, at high speed of an electric mixer, until foamy; add sugar and vanilla, and beat, until soft peaks form. Spread evenly over pie filling. In a small saucepan, combine chocolate morsels and milk; cook, over low heat, until chocolate melts (stir constantly). Drizzle chocolate mixture over whipped cream; sprinkle with remaining ¼ cup pecans. Chill for several hours. Makes 9 servings.

* Other pie fillings (ex.: cherry) can be substituted, if desired.

Fredrick W. "Fred" & Shay Strickland, Jr.

Linebacker

6′2″
251 lbs.

Philosophy to Live by

"Always treat people the way you would want to be treated." — *Fred*
"If everything else has failed, always look to God." — *Shay*

Fred and Shay Strickland

Best Advice I Could Give to a High School Senior

"Stay in school, and pursue your dreams." —*Fred*

"Get an education, and try to stay away from the bad things in life." — *Shay*

What I Value Most

"A relationship with God, and our marriage." —*Fred and Shay*

Best Asset

"Making people to feel comfortable." —*Fred*
"My ability to get along with people." — *Shay*

BORN

Fred - 8-15-66

Shay - 9-26-65

COLLEGE

Fred - Purdue

Shay - Purdue

YEARS IN NFL

10th Year

Dallas Cowboys (2)

Los Angeles Rams (5)

Minnesota Vikings (1)

Green Bay Packers (2)

SPOUSE'S OCCUPATION

Doctor's assistant

ANNIVERSARY

May 28 - 3 years

PETS

Sinbad & Prince - Rottweilers

Biggest Challenge Ever Faced in Life

"Making a marriage work." —*Fred*

If I Were Not in Professional Football I Would Be

"A football coach." —*Fred*

Game Day Rituals

"Listening to music." —*Fred*

Favorite Pre-Game or Post-Game Meal

Pre-game - "Eggs, bacon, and sausage." —*Fred*

Fred and Shay Strickland

Favorite Holiday or Holiday Tradition

"Christmas, and Fourth of July." —*Fred and Shay*

Favorite City outside of Dallas

"New York City." —*Fred*

"Atlanta, Georgia, and New York City." — *Shay*

Hobbies and Other Interests

"Riding my Harley." —*Fred*

"Riding with my husband on our Harley." — *Shay*

Apple Cherry Cobbler

1 egg, beaten
½ cup sugar
½ cup milk
2 tablespoons vegetable oil
1 cup all-purpose flour
1¼ teaspoons baking powder
1 can (21-ounce) apple pie filling
1 can (21-ounce) cherry pie filling
1 tablespoon lemon juice
1 teaspoon vanilla

TOPPING:

⅓ cup packed brown sugar
3 tablespoons all-purpose flour
1 teaspoon ground cinnamon
2 tablespoons butter

In a bowl, combine egg, sugar, milk, and vegetable oil. Combine flour and baking powder; add to egg mixture. Blend well; pour into a greased 13" x 9" x 2" baking pan. Combine apple and cherry pie fillings, lemon juice, and vanilla; spoon over batter. For topping: combine all ingredients; sprinkle over filling. Bake at 350 degrees for 40 to 45 minutes, or until bubbly and cake tests done. If necessary, cover edges with foil (to prevent over-browning). Top with whipped cream (or vanilla ice cream) before serving. Makes 12 to 16 servings.

Most Memorable Moment in Life outside of Pro-Football

"The day we got married." —*Fred and Shay*

Favorite Time of Day and Why

"Afternoon - most relaxing part of the day." —*Fred*
"Morning - because it's a new day." —*Shay*

Orange Muffins

1 cup raisins
1 cup sugar
½ cup butter, softened
2 tablespoons sour cream
2 eggs
2 cups all-purpose flour
¼ teaspoon salt
1 teaspoon baking soda
⅔ cup buttermilk
2 teaspoons finely-shredded orange peel

Grease eighteen 2½-inch muffin cups, or line them with paper bake cups; set muffin cups aside. Place raisins in a food processor bowl; cover, and process raisins, until finely-chopped (or, use a knife to chop finely); set raisins aside. In a medium mixing bowl, beat sugar, butter, and sour cream with an electric mixture, on medium to high speed, until fluffy; beat in eggs. In a small mixing bowl, stir together flour and salt; add flour mixture to butter mixture, beating, on low speed, just till combined. Stir baking soda into buttermilk; stir this into mixture just combined. Fold in chopped raisins and orange peel. Spoon batter into the prepared muffin cups, filling each two-thirds full. Bake at 400 degrees for 14 to 15 minutes, or till a toothpick inserted near each center comes out clean. Immediately brush the hot muffin tops with the Orange Glaze. Makes 18 muffins.

Orange Glaze: In a small bowl, stir together ⅓ cup sugar and ¼ cup orange juice. Makes approximately ⅓ cup.

Nicky Sualua

45

Fullback

5′11″
257 lbs.

BORN
4-15-75

COLLEGE
Ohio State

YEARS IN NFL
Rookie

Best Advice I Could Give to a High School Senior

"Know what you want to do, and stick with it." — *Nicky*

© James D. Smith Photography

Nicky Sualua - stands to become the heaviest player in the Cowboys' backfield since the early 1990's

What I Value Most

"My family." — *Nicky*

Best Asset

"I'm quiet, and I listen." — *Nicky*

Game Day Rituals

"Try to listen to music." — *Nicky*

My Last Meal Would Be

"Eggs - my favorite food." — *Nicky*

Favorite Childhood Snack

"Chips." — *Nicky*

Hobbies and Other Interests

"I like to play games—video games, card games, or dominoes; and listening to music (Reggae and a lot of oldies)." — *Nicky*

Jalapeno Cornbread Muffins

1 cup yellow cornmeal
½ teaspoon salt
1 tablespoon baking powder
⅓ cup melted shortening
2 large eggs, beaten
1 cup cream-style canned corn
⅔ cup buttermilk
1 medium onion, chopped
1 cup shredded sharp Cheddar cheese
1 can (4-ounce) chopped green chilies, drained

Preheat oven to 350 degrees. Lightly oil a muffin tin (for 12 muffins). In a large bowl, combine cornmeal, salt, and baking powder. Stir in shortening. Add eggs, creamed corn, and buttermilk; blend well. Stir in chopped onion. Fill each muffin cup with 2 to 3 tablespoons butter. Sprinkle on the cheese and jalapenos; top each with a smooth layer of remaining batter. Bake for 35 to 40 minutes, or until a toothpick inserted in the center of each muffin comes out clean. Let muffins cool before removing from the cups. Makes 12 muffins.

Broderick Thomas

Defensive End

6′4″
254 lbs.

BORN

2-20-67

COLLEGE

Nebraska

YEARS IN NFL

9th Year

Dallas Cowboys (2)

Minnesota Vikings (1)

Detroit Lions (1)

Tampa Bay (5)

CHILDREN

Broderic, Jr. - 7 years

Advice I Could Give to a High School Senior

"Pray to God, and listen to your parents and your elders." — *Broderick*

Broderick Thomas - has great pass rushing ability

Philosophy to Live by

"God's rules." — *Broderick*

What I Value Most

"Family." — *Broderick*

Best Asset

"God." — *Broderick*

Biggest Challenge Ever Faced in Life

"Getting away from street life." — *Broderick*

If I Were Not in Professional Football I Would Be

"Working in the social work field." — *Broderick*

The Cowboys plan on Thomas being an integral part of the Cowboys' defensive end rotation

Three People I Would Invite to a "Fantasy" Dinner Party
"Jamie Foxx, Tommy Davidson, and Anita Baker." — *Broderick*

Former Cowboys Player/Coach Most Admired and Why
"Drew Pearson - carried himself with class and dignity; a great role model." — *Broderick*

Game Day Rituals
"Read Philippians 4:13." — *Broderick*

Favorite Pre-Game or Post-Game Meal
"Two baked potatoes with Ranch dressing, and a lot of water." — *Broderick*

My Last Meal Would Be
"Porterhouse steak from Nebraska, baked potato, and salad with Ranch dressing." — *Broderick*

Favorite Childhood Snack
"Cookies." — *Broderick*

Favorite Holiday or Holiday Tradition
"Thanksgiving." — *Broderick*

Favorite City outside of Dallas

"Houston, Texas." — *Broderick*

Hobbies and Other Interests

"Drag racing." — *Broderick*

Most Memorable Moment in Life outside of Pro Football

"Hanging out with high school classmates." — *Broderick*

Favorite Time of Day and Why

"Night - because my blood gets warm." — *Broderick*

Fresh Corn Pudding

6 ears fresh sweet corn, shucked
½ cup heavy cream
½ cup milk
1 tablespoon sugar
½ teaspoon salt
⅛ teaspoon freshly-ground white pepper
4 tablespoons unsalted butter, melted
3 large eggs

Preheat the oven to 350 degrees. Butter a 1½-quart casserole. Grate the fresh corn into a bowl, catching all of the kernels and liquid. With a teaspoon, scrape the cobs (to remove all of the pulp and liquid). Add the cream, milk, sugar, salt, and pepper. Stir in the butter. Beat the eggs together, until light and lemon-colored; add them to the corn mixture. Stir, to combine thoroughly. Pour the pudding into the prepared casserole; set the casserole in a baking pan. Add hot water to reach halfway up the side of the casserole. Bake for 1 hour, or until set and firm. Serve hot. Makes 6 servings.

Anthony Lewis "Tony" & Satasha "Tasha" Tolbert

Biggest Challenge Ever Faced in Life

"Coming back after three surgeries." — *Tony*

"Watching my mother get sick with a brain tumor. She's much, much better now. Thank God!" — *Tasha*

Tony and Tasha Tolbert - in Hawaii for the '97 Pro Bowl

Philosophy to Live by

"To each his own, I guess." — *Tony*

"Trust in God—not in man." — *Tasha*

Best Advice I Could Give to a High School Senior

"Respect yourself and others." — *Tony*

"Learn all you can about computers, life, and respect yourself and others." — *Tasha*

What I Value Most

"Family." — *Tony and Tasha*

All-Pro Defensive End

6′6″
263 lbs.

BORN

Tony - 12-29-67

Tasha - 3-29-68

COLLEGE

Tony - Texas - El Paso

Tasha - Texas - El Paso

YEARS IN NFL

9th Year

Dallas Cowboys

ANNIVERSARY

September 24 - 4 years

SPOUSE'S OCCUPATION

Mother and wife

CHILDREN

Anthony, Jr. "AJ" - 2 years

Best Asset

"Having the Lord in my life." — *Tasha*

If I Were Not in Professional Football I Would Be

"Wherever life takes me." — *Tony*

Two People I Would Invite to a "Fantasy" Dinner Party

"Muhammad Ali and Richard Pryor." — *Tony*

Former Cowboys Player/Coach Most Admired & Why

"Steve Telander - taught me about football and some aspect of life." — *Tony*

Anthony Tolbert, Jr.

Game Day Rituals

"Rush around getting AJ and I dressed - nothing special!" — *Tasha*

Favorite Pre-Game or Post-Game Meal

Pre-Game - "Chicken and pasta, or eggs and waffles." — *Tony*

My Last Meal Would Be

"Anything my mom would cook." — *Tony*
"Anything my mom would cook." — *Tasha*

Favorite Childhood Snack

"Any type of cookies." — *Tony*

"Peanut butter and pickles." — *Tasha*

Favorite Holiday or Holiday Tradition

"Thanksgiving - family time; and Labor Day - start of the season." — *Tony*

"Thanksgiving - both families come together and eat at my house." — *Tasha*

Favorite City outside of Dallas

"New York City." — *Tony*

"San Francisco, California." — *Tasha*

Hobbies and Other Interests

"Music, other sports, and shopping." — *Tony*

"Working out, nutrition, and hanging out with Tony." — *Tasha*

Most Memorable Moment in Life outside of Pro-Football

"AJ's birth." — *Tony*

"Having AJ." — *Tasha*

Favorite Time of Day and Why

"Night time - sleep is around the corner." — *Tony*

"Evening - I can get things done without the little one, or just watch TV." — *Tasha*

"AJ" - 20 months

Conna's Corn Dip

2 blocks (8-ounce) of cream cheese (Neufchatel or non-fat is fine)
2 cans (15-ounce) of corn
2 sticks of butter (can use reduced-fat margarine)

In saucepan, melt butter and cream cheese together. Add corn. Stir, and mix, until blended. Serve with corn chips. Enjoy!

* This dip is very rich. You can reduce the amount of butter to 1 or 1½ sticks.

Flounder Grilled in Foil

4 to 6 pounds flounder (or other types of fish, such as red snapper, trout, or fish fillets of any kind)
¼ cup freshly-squeezed lemon juice
½ cup thinly-sliced onion
4 to 6 stalks celery, chopped
6 medium-size ripe tomatoes, sliced
1 large green pepper, cut into strips
4 carrots, thinly-sliced
4 tablespoons freshly-squeezed lemon juice
4 to 6 lemon wedges
butter
salt, to taste

Cut 4 to 6 squares heavy-duty aluminum foil. Sprinkle lemon over flounder; then, cut fish into 4 to 6 serving-size pieces. Put a serving of fish on each square of aluminum foil. On each piece of fish, put sliced onion, chopped celery, sliced tomato, pepper strips, sliced carrots, lemon juice, and lemon wedges. Put a dot of butter on each stack; add salt, to taste. Seal packets securely. Lay on grill, over medium heat. Turn packets every 15 minutes; cook, until fish flakes easily (about 35 minutes). Makes 4 to 6 servings.

Mark Pulemau "Tui" & Ponolani "Pono" Tuinei

All-Pro Tackle

6'5"
314 lbs.

Best Advice I Could Give to a High School Senior

"Work hard - nothing will come easy." — *Mark*
"Do the very best in your studies, and prepare yourself for college - college will be the best time of your life." — *Pono*

Mark Tuinei and his mom, Ane (February, 1997)

Philosophy to Live by

"Don't judge a book by its cover, and do unto others as you would have done unto you."
— *Pono*

BORN

Mark - 3-31-60

Pono - 2-25

COLLEGE

Mark - UCLA & Hawaii

Pono - Santa Ana College

YEARS IN NFL

15th Year

Dallas Cowboys

SPOUSE'S OCCUPATION

Partner in business in Hawaii - Kidsports

ANNIVERSARY

February 19 - 14 years in 1998

PETS

Shaka Zulu - Rottweiler

Lil' Mama - Llasa Apso

What I Value Most

"Life, happiness, and good company." — *Mark*

"Family and friends - knowing their lives are safe and sound, and my relationship with God." — *Pono*

Mark - taking a swing!

Best Asset

Pono's opinion of Mark's "best" would be: "Commitment to work; a 'company man' with teammates' respect."

Mark thinks Pono's "best" would be: "Her singing - recalling way back to first date, where she sang a few songs with a friend's band."

Biggest Challenge Ever Faced in Life

"Recovering from an automobile accident as a child - I was struck by a car and hurt badly (thanks be to God!)." — *Pono*

If I Were Not in Professional Football I Would Be

"My hobby in college was working on cars - I'd like to own a mechanical shop." — *Mark*

Three People We Would Invite to a "Fantasy" Dinner Party

"Vanessa Williams, Muhammad Ali, and
Bernice Panahi Bishop (founder of Pono's school -
K-12 grades - The Kamehameha Schools)." — *Mark and Pono*

Pono (second from right) - with friends at Vikings' game (1996)

Former Cowboys Player/Coach Most Admired and Why

"Randy White - he really had good work habits, and was one of the greats." — *Mark*

Game Day Rituals

"I like to arrive early, conserve energy, prepare slowly and deliberately, and focus on job duty." — *Mark*

"Panic, pray for protection, and . . .
(*Mark chimed in with:* 'try on 4 outfits'! Ha!)." — *Pono*

My Last Meal Would Be

"Surf-n-Turf (steak and lobster)." — *Mark*

"Squid luau - opihi and poi ale are Hawaiian delicacies." — *Pono*

Mark Tuinei's mom, Ane - as a child

Favorite Childhood Snack

"Manapua (Chinese dumpling) and mayonnaise sandwiches (yum!)." — *Mark*

"Ice cream on Sundays after church." — *Pono*

Favorite Holiday or Holiday Tradition

"New Year's Day." — *Mark*

"Valentine's Day, and Easter." — *Pono*

Hillary Hellestrae thinks her "pretend" Uncle Mark and Aunty Pono are goofy! - taken at Joe T. Garcia's (December, 1996)

Favorite City outside of Dallas

"Honolulu, Hawaii." — *Mark and Pono*

Hobbies and Other Interests

"Golf, pool, darts, and cards." — *Mark*

"Music (singing), working out, concerts, and musical theater." — *Pono*

Most Memorable Moment in Life outside of Pro-Football

"My wedding day." — *Mark*

"Winning the talent and evening gown competitions in the Miss Hawaii Scholarship Pageant." — *Pono*

Favorite Time of Day and Why

"Bedtime - peace and quiet." — *Mark*

"Evening - nothing beats a remarkable sunset." — *Pono*

Miracle Bars

½ cup butter
1½ cups graham cracker crumbs
1 can (14 ounces) sweet condensed milk
6 ounces chocolate chips
1⅓ cups coconut, shredded
1 cup nuts, chopped (I like walnuts!)

Preheat oven to 350 degrees. Melt butter in 13" x 9" pan. Sprinkle crumbs over butter. Add milk; top with remaining ingredients. Press firmly. Bake for 25 to 30 minutes. Cool; cut in squares.

* Serve with Haagen-daz and coffee!

Impossible Taco Pie

3 pounds ground beef
1½ cups chopped onion
3 envelopes Taco Seasoning Mix
3 cans (4-ounce) chopped green chilies, drained
3¾ cups milk
2¼ cups Bisquick
9 eggs
6 tomatoes, sliced
3 cups shredded Monterrey Jack or Cheddar cheese

* (Recipe of Mark's mom, Ane)

Heat oven to 400 degrees. Grease pan. Cook and stir beef and onion, until brown; drain. Stir in seasoning mix. Spread in pan; top with chilies. Beat milk, Bisquick, and eggs, until smooth; pour into plate. Bake for 25 minutes. Top with tomatoes and cheese. Bake, until knife inserted in center comes out clean (8 to 10 minutes longer). Cool for 5 minutes. Serve with sour cream, chopped tomatoes, shredded lettuce, and shredded cheese, if desired. Makes 6 to 8 servings.

Herschel & Cindy Walker

Running Back

6'1"
225 lbs.

Favorite Time of Day and Why

"Morning - it is the start of a brand new day - I feel blessed to be alive." — *Herschel.*

"Morning - it is a happy time - a time to face the challenges of the day." — *Cindy*

Cindy and Herschel Walker

Philosophy to Live by

"The Lord will lay a path down - all you have to do is follow it." — *Herschel*

Best Advice I Could Give to a High School Senior

"Be the best you can be at all times." — *Herschel*

"Always give your best in whatever you do." — *Cindy*

What I Value Most

"My love for Jesus Christ." — *Herschel*

"My faith in Jesus Christ." — *Cindy*

BORN

Herschel - 3-3-62

Cindy - 9-4

COLLEGE

Herschel - Georgia

Cindy - Georgia

YEARS IN NFL

12th Year

Dallas Cowboys (5)

Minnesota Vikings (3)

Philadelphia Eagles (3)

New York Giants (1)

SPOUSE'S OCCUPATION

Housewife

ANNIVERSARY

March 3 - 14 years

PETS

Al Capone - Rottweiler

Best Asset

"Friendliness." — *Herschel*

"Loyalty." — *Cindy*

Biggest Challenge Ever Faced in Life

"The deaths of my brother and nephew." — *Herschel*

"My mother's bout with breast cancer." — *Cindy*

If I Were Not in Professional Football I Would Be

"In the F.B.I." — *Herschel*

Three People I Would Invite to a "Fantasy" Dinner Party

"Jesus Christ, Martin Luther King, and Mother Teresa." — *Herschel*

Former Cowboys Player/Coach Most Admired and Why

"Coach Landry - I admire his stand for Christ." — *Herschel*

Herschel Walker - what a catch!

Game Day Rituals

"Pray a lot." — *Cindy*

Favorite Pre-Game or Post-Game Meal

Post-Game - "Fried chicken, blackeyed peas, and bread." — *Herschel*

My Last Meal Would Be

"Caesar salad, Capellini Romodoro, lobster, and creme brulee." — *Cindy*

Favorite Childhood Snack
"Tea cakes/cookies." — *Herschel*

"Ice cream and candy/cookies." — *Cindy*

Favorite Holiday or Holiday Tradition
"Christmas." — *Herschel and Cindy*

Favorite City outside of Dallas
"Atlanta, Georgia." — *Herschel*

"New York City." — *Cindy*

Riding horses is one of Herschel's favorite activities

Hobbies and Other Interests
"Riding my Harley, Tae-kwon-do, working out, going to movies, and riding horses." — *Herschel*

"Lifting weights, tennis, running, Bible study, and cooking." — *Cindy*

Most Memorable Moment in Life outside of Pro-Football
"My marriage." — *Herschel and Cindy*

Minestrone Soup

½ pound dry white beans, soaked in water overnight
3 quarts salted water
1 teaspoon olive oil
⅛ pound salt pork, diced
1 clove garlic, finely chopped
1 small onion, chopped
1 leek, diced and washed
1 teaspoon chopped basil
1 tablespoon tomato paste
3 tomatoes, peeled, seeded, and chopped
3 stalks celery, chopped
2 carrots, sliced
2 potatoes, sliced
1 small turnip, diced
¼ small cabbage, shredded
2 zucchini, diced
1½ quarts water
½ teaspoon black pepper
1 cup elbow macaroni
6 tablespoons grated Parmesan cheese

Drain the beans (that have soaked overnight); boil them in the salted water about 1 hour, or until tender. Drain. Place the olive oil in a large kettle; add the salt pork, garlic, onion, leek, parsley, and basil. Brown lightly. Add the tomato paste, thinned with a little water, and cook for 5 minutes. Add the tomatoes, celery, carrots, potatoes, turnip, cabbage, zucchini, water, salt, and pepper; cook slowly for 45 minutes to 1 hour. Add the beans. Add elbow macaroni; cook for 10 minutes, or until tender. Correct the seasonings, and serve immediately. Sprinkle with Parmesan cheese.

Kenny Wheaton

Cornerback

5′10″
190 lbs.

BORN
3-8-75

COLLEGE
Oregon

YEARS IN NFL
Rookie

Philosophy to Live by

"One day at a time." — *Kenny*

Kenny Wheaton - a Sociology major in college - is the third defensive back that Dallas has drafted from Oregon

Best Advice I Could Give to a High School Senior

"Go to college." — *Kenny*

What I Value Most

"Family." — *Kenny*

Best Asset

"Car." — *Kenny*

Biggest Challenge Ever Faced in Life

"N. F. L." — *Kenny*

If I Were Not in Professional Football I Would Be

"Youth worker." — *Kenny*

Three People I Would Invite to a "Fantasy" Dinner Party
"Halle Berry, Vivica Fox, and Janet Jackson." — *Kenny*

Game Day Rituals
"Relaxing." — *Kenny*

Favorite Pre-Game or Post-Game Meal
"Pasta." — *Kenny*

My Last Meal Would Be
"Barbecue." — *Kenny*

Favorite Childhood Snack
"Honey bar." — *Kenny*

Favorite Holiday or Holiday Tradition
"Thanksgiving." — *Kenny*

Favorite City outside of Dallas
"Phoenix, Arizona." — *Kenny*

Hobbies and Other Interests
"Shopping." — *Kenny*

Most Memorable Moment in Life outside of Pro-Football
"Rose Bowl." — *Kenny*

Favorite Time of Day and Why
"Evening - your day is over." — *Kenny*

Pumpkin Pie in Spiced Nut Crust

SPICED NUT CRUST

1 cup all-purpose flour
½ cup finely-chopped pecans
¼ cup firmly-packed light brown sugar
¼ cup, plus 2 tablespoons, butter, melted
½ teaspoon ground cinnamon
20 pecan halves

FILLING

1 can (16-ounce) pumpkin
1 can (14-ounce) sweetened condensed milk
2 eggs, beaten
1 teaspoon ground cinnamon
½ teaspoon ground ginger
½ teaspoon ground nutmeg
¼ teaspoon salt
whipped cream or spray can of whipped topping

For crust: Combine all ingredients, except pecan halves; stir well. Press onto bottom and sides of a 9-inch pie plate. Press pecan halves onto the rim of the crust at one-inch intervals. Makes one 9-inch pie shell.

For filling: Combine pumpkin, condensed milk, cinnamon, ginger, nutmeg, and salt; stir well. Pour into crust; bake at 350 degrees for 50 to 55 minutes, or until set. Remove from oven; let cool. Place whipped cream, or spray whipped topping, on top before serving. Makes one 9-inch pie.

Charlie Williams

What I Value Most

"My family." — *Charlie*

Safety

6'0"
189 lbs.

BORN

2-2-72

COLLEGE

Bowling Green State

YEARS IN NFL

3rd Year

Dallas Cowboys

Charlie Williams - has proven to be a significant contributor on Dallas' special teams units

Favorite City outside of Dallas

"Las Vegas, Nevada." — *Charlie*

Hobbies and Other Interests

"Reading comic books." — *Charlie*

French Dip Sandwiches

1 lean beef roast (3 to 4 pounds)
½ cup soy sauce
1 beef bouillon cube
1 bay leaf
4 whole peppercorns
1 teaspoon dried crushed rosemary
1 teaspoon dried thyme
1 teaspoon garlic powder
hard rolls, or French bread

Remove and discard all visible fat from roast. Place roast in a slow cooker. Combine soy sauce, bouillon, and spices; pour over roast. Add water (almost to cover roast). Cover, and cook, over low heat, for 10 to 12 hours, or until meat is very tender. Remove meat from broth; reserve broth. Shred meat with a fork. Serve on hard rolls, or French bread slices, with broth. Makes 12 sandwiches.

Awesome Brownies

½ cup butter
2 squares unsweetened chocolate
1 cup sugar
2 eggs
½ cup flour
1 cup chopped pecans
½ teaspoon vanilla

FROSTING

1 cup sugar
¼ cup butter
¼ cup milk
¼ cup cocoa

Preheat oven to 350 degrees. Melt butter and chocolate in a double boiler. When melted, remove from heat; add sugar, and beat well. Add eggs (one at a time), beating after each addition. Add flour, nuts, and vanilla; mix well. Pour into a greased and floured 9" x 9" pan. Bake for 20 to 25 minutes (*do not bake too long - they are supposed to be moist*).

For frosting: Mix together all ingredients; bring to a full boil, over low heat, stirring constantly. Cook exactly 1 minute - *no longer.* Remove from heat; cool, stir, and frost. Let frosting harden before cutting brownies.

Erik George Williams

All-Pro Tackle

What I Value Most

"Parents, and children." — *Erik*

6′6″
328 lbs.

BORN
9-7-68

COLLEGE
Central State (OH)

CHILDREN
Shi - 6 years

YEARS IN NFL
7th Year
Dallas Cowboys

Erik Williams - one of the top young offensive linemen in the NFL

Biggest Challenge Ever Faced in Life

"Knee surgery." — *Erik*

If I Were Not in Professional Football I Would Be

"Wrestler." — *Erik*

Three People I Would Invite to a "Fantasy" Dinner Party

"Mother, father, and daughter." — *Erik*

Game Day Rituals

"Dip mouth piece in Gatorade." — *Erik*

My Last Meal Would Be
"Chicken." — *Erik*

Favorite Childhood Snack
"Cheese." — *Erik*

Favorite Holiday or Holiday Tradition
"Christmas." — *Erik*

Most Memorable Moment in Life outside of Pro-Football
"When daughter was born." — *Erik*

Favorite Time of Day and Why
"Night - sleep." — *Erik*

Erik - after suffering a season-ending knee injury, completed his return to the top as one of the NFL's greatest right tackles

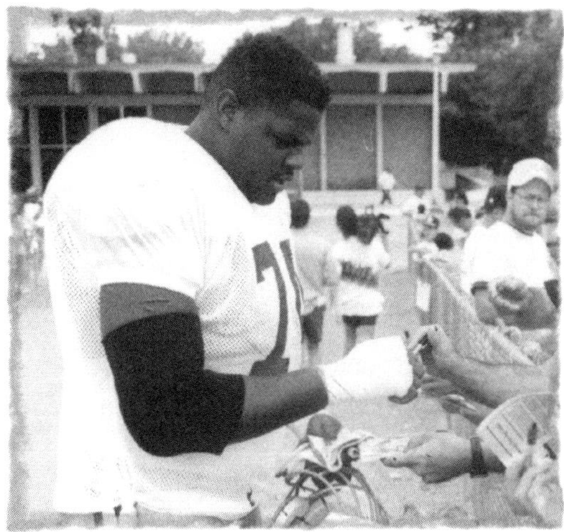

Erik - making the fans happy - signing autographs!

Baked Beans Western-Style

1 pound pinto beans
6 cups water
½ cup chopped onions
1 tablespoon vegetable oil
1 can tomatoes and chilies
3 tablespoons brown sugar
pinch of oregano
1 teaspoon salt
⅛ teaspoon pepper

Soak beans overnight; drain. Cook beans in boiling water, until tender (add water, if needed). Pour beans into a casserole. Sauté onions in the oil, until tender; stir in tomatoes and chilies, brown sugar, oregano, salt, and pepper. Then, stir into beans. Cover, and bake at 325 degrees for 30 minutes. Uncover, and bake for 30 minutes longer. Makes 8 to 10 servings.

Barbecued Pork Chops

pork chops
salt and pepper
1 large onion, diced
¼ cup catsup
½ cup Worcestershire sauce
1 can (10½-ounce) condensed tomato soup
1 soup can of water
¼ cup vinegar
½ tablespoon sugar
dash of pepper
1¼ teaspoon salt
1 clove garlic, minced
½ tablespoon butter

Mix all ingredients (except pork chops, and salt and pepper) together; place in deep big Dutch oven. Salt and pepper pork chops; drop into sauce. Cover, and cook at 325 degrees for 2 hours.

*There's enough sauce to bake several pork chops, if you like.

Sherman Williams

Running Back

5′8″
202 lbs.

BORN
8-13-73

COLLEGE
Alabama

CHILDREN
Sherman, Jr. - 7 years
Kristian - 5 years

YEARS IN NFL
3rd Year
Dallas Cowboys

Best Advice I Could Give to a High School Senior

"Always have respect for others." — *Sherman*

Sherman Williams - a very reliable running back, with powerful legs and great field instinct

What I Value Most

"My family." — *Sherman*

Favorite City outside of Dallas

"Miami, Florida." — *Sherman*

Crab Bake Sandwich

1 pound fresh lump white crabmeat
1 hard-boiled egg, grated
3 ribs celery, chopped
20 green stuffed olives, chopped
juice of 1 lemon
¼ cup mayonnaise
⅛ teaspoon cayenne pepper
salt and pepper, to taste
English muffins
avocado, optional
tomato slices, optional
Monterrey Jack cheese

Rinse crabmeat several times, carefully removing any bone or fin that has been left in the meat; drain, and squeeze out excess liquid. Stir together the crabmeat, egg, celery, olives, lemon juice, mayonnaise, cayenne pepper, and salt and black pepper; chill. Spread muffin halves with butter; toast. Place avocado and/or tomato slices on muffin halves. Cover with a mound of crabmeat mixture; top with sliced or grated Monterrey Jack cheese. Place under broiler, until cheese has melted and begins to brown. Makes 4 to 6 servings (two halves to each serving).

French Chocolate

2½ squares unsweetened chocolate (1-ounce package)
½ cup water
⅔ cup sugar
½ teaspoon salt
½ cup whipping cream, whipped
1 quart milk, piping hot

In a saucepan, combine chocolate and water; cook, over low heat (stirring), until chocolate melts. Add sugar and salt; bring to a boil. Reduce the heat; simmer for 4 minutes. Cool, to room temperature; fold in whipped cream. Place 1 heaping tablespoon of the chocolate mixture in each cup; fill cups with hot milk. Stir, and serve.

Stepfret Ornell Williams, Jr.

80

Wide Receiver

What I Value Most

"The love and guidance of Jesus Christ, and my family and friends." — *Stepfret*

6'0"
170 lbs.

BORN

6-14-73

COLLEGE

Northeast Louisiana

YEARS IN NFL

2nd Year

Dallas Cowboys

CHILDREN

Jordan Marshall - 2 years

Stepfret - with sister (Stepfionne), daughter (Jordan), and brother (Stepfon)

Philosophy to Live by

"Keep God first in your life and trust Him, through the power of the Holy Spirit, to lead you to do the right things." — *Stepfret*

Best Advice I Could Give to a High School Senior

"Continue your education, stay focused, and don't let the trials of life prevent you from achieving your goals." — *Stepfret*

Best Asset

"Strong work ethics, and humility." — *Stepfret*

Biggest Challenge Ever Faced in Life

"Leaving my family in Louisiana to live on my own as a professional athlete, and striving to do all I need to do in order to be successful." — *Stepfret*

If I Were Not in Professional Football I Would Be

"An accountant." — *Stepfret*

Three People I Would Invite to a "Fantasy" Dinner Party

"Jerry Rice, Michael Jordan, and my dad." — *Stepfret*

Stepfret - with sister and brother, Aunt Yvette, Uncle Wyman, and cousins

Former Cowboys Player/Coach Most Admired and Why

"Drew Pearson, Tony Hill, and Tony Dorsett - they were great players!" — *Stepfret*

Game Day Rituals

"I wear a T-shirt—with a biblical scripture or thought on it—under my game jersey." — *Stepfret*

Favorite Pre-Game or Post-Game Meal

"Steak, potatoes, and corn." — *Stepfret*

Stepfret and his Aunt Yvette

My Last Meal Would Be

"Chicken breast and fries." — *Stepfret*

Favorite Childhood Snack

"Hamburger and fries." — *Stepfret*

Favorite Holiday or Holiday Tradition

"Opening gifts on Christmas morning with my brother and sister." — *Stepfret*

Favorite City outside of Dallas

"Minden, Louisiana - home." — *Stepfret*

Hobbies and Other Interests

"Playing video games, and learning to play golf." — *Stepfret*

Most Memorable Moment in Life outside of Pro-Football

"Graduating from high school, and signing my scholarship to attend NLU." — *Stepfret*

Favorite Time of Day and Why

"The time spent practicing in the receiver position, because I hope to develop into a very skillful receiver." — *Stepfret*

Crawfish Fettucine

½ stick margarine
6 to 8 green onions, chopped
1 quart half-and-half milk
2 pounds crawfish, chopped in large pieces

Sauté green onions in margarine, over medium heat, until transparent. Add half-and-half milk; turn heat up (stir constantly) until the sauce is thick. Add crawfish. Boil fettucine, according to package directions. Serve sauce over fettucine, or mix together, if desired; serve.

* May use angel hair pasta.

Coconut Pie

2 eggs
1 cup Pet milk
1 teaspoon flour
1 cup sugar
1 can angel-flake coconut
1 teaspoon vanilla
½ stick butter, melted
unbaked pie shell
whipping cream, whipped

Pour milk over coconut; let stand. Beat eggs; add sugar, mixed with flour. Add coconut and milk to the other ingredients. Add vanilla and melted butter. Pour into uncooked pie shell. Bake at 325 degrees, until done (about 30 minutes). When pie has cooled, put whipped cream on top. Refrigerate, until served.

Charles "Wade" & Kathy Wilson

Quarterback

6′3″
208 lbs.

Philosophy to Live by

"Keep everything in the proper perspective." — *Wade*
"Treat others the way you would want to be treated." — *Kathy*

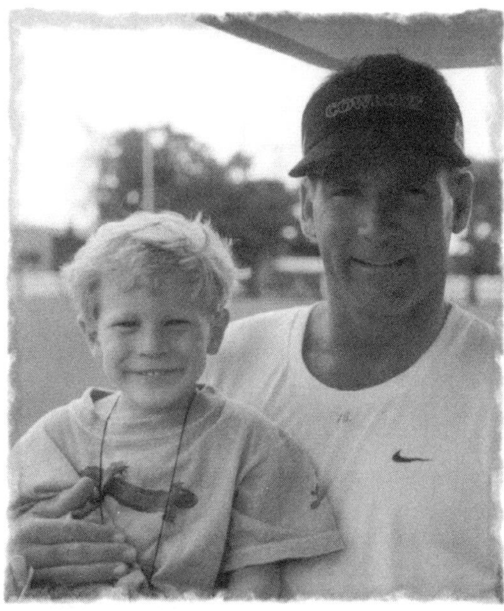

Wade Wilson - with son, Hayden

BORN

Wade - 2-1-59

Kathy - 10-3-59

COLLEGE

Wade - East Texas State

Kathy - Oklahoma

YEARS IN NFL

17th Year - Dallas Cowboys (3)

New Orleans Saints (2)

Atlanta Falcons (1)

Minnesota Vikings (11)

SPOUSE'S OCCUPATION

M.O.M.

ANNIVERSARY

April 16 -14 years

CHILDREN

Travis Wade - 7 years

Hayden Lee - 4 years

Twins: Sophie Kathryn & Coleton Dale - 1 year

What I Value Most

"My family." — *Wade*

"My children, and the time I spend with them." — *Kathy*

Best Asset

"Focus and drive." — *Wade*

"Having patience with my children." — *Kathy*

Biggest Challenge Ever Faced in Life

"Diabetes." — *Wade*

"When my children begin driving - will be learning to deal with my anxiety." — *Kathy*

Three People I Would Invite to a "Fantasy" Dinner Party

"Clint Eastwood, Joe Namath, and Gene Hackman." — *Wade*

Former Cowboys Player/Coach Most Admired and Why

"Roger Staubach - for his strong character qualities." — *Kathy*

Game Day Rituals

"Bill Bates pulls on my jersey." — *Wade*

My Last Meal Would Be

"Chicken fried steak." — *Wade*

Favorite Childhood Snack

"Popcorn." — *Wade*

"Cheetos, or Tootsie Rolls." — *Kathy*

Favorite Holiday or Holiday Tradition

"Christmas." — *Wade and Kathy*

Kathy Wilson - holding Cole (July, 1997)

Hobbies and Other Interests

"Photography, reading, traveling, and movies with friends." — *Kathy*

Most Memorable Moment in Life outside of Pro-Football

"Birth of my children." — *Wade and Kathy*

Wilson children: Travis, Cole, Sophie, and Hayden (July, 1997)

Chicken Pot Pie

2 cans Campbell's cream of chicken soup
1 pound Bird'seye frozen mixed vegetables
3 or 4 chicken breast halves (bone in, with skin)
½ cup chicken broth
black pepper
2 Ritz pie crusts

Stew chicken, covered, until tender (about 1 hour). Meanwhile, put vegetables in large Corning Ware dish; microwave, on high, for 4 minutes, covered. When chicken is done, remove skin and bones; cut into bite-size chunks. Add to vegetables, along with soup, broth, and pepper. Bake for 30 to 45 minutes at 400 degrees, covered (*should be bubbling when done*). About 10 minutes before done, bake pie crusts for about 9 minutes at 450 degrees. Take all out of oven; break up crust into large pieces. Punch pieces down into the chicken mixture.

* Note: It helps if you take chicken mixture out about halfway through cooking, and stir it away from sides of dish.
* Travis and Hayden *love* this recipe!!!

Chocolate Layered Dessert

8 ounces cream cheese
1 cup powdered sugar
1 container (12-ounce) Cool Whip
3½ cups cold milk
Ghirardelli or Hershey chocolate bar
1 stick butter
1 cup flour
1 small package Jell-O Instant Chocolate Pudding Mix
1 small package Jell-O Instant Vanilla Pudding Mix
1 cup finely-ground pecans

Mix flour and butter; add pecans. Press mixture into 13" x 9" baking dish. Bake for 20 minutes at 375 degrees. Let cool. Beat cream cheese and powdered sugar, until smooth. Stir in half of the container of Cool Whip (6 ounces). Spread onto cooled crust (*to ease spreading, crust should be very cold*); set aside. In mixing bowl, combine cold milk with chocolate and vanilla pudding mixes; beat, on low speed, for 2 minutes. Pour and spread over cream cheese layer. Spread remainder of Cool Whip on top. Garnish with grated (or curled) chocolate bar.

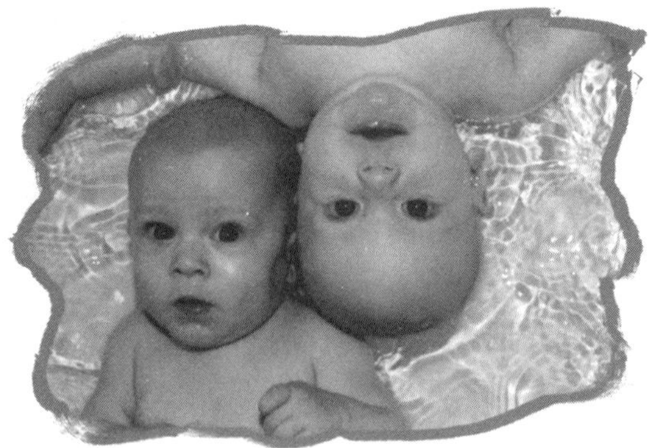

"Double-Take" - Wilson twins, Sophie and Cole (June, 1997)

Darren Ray & Juli Woodson

All-Pro Safety

6′1″
219 lbs.

Philosophy to Live by

"Always be yourself, and be true to others." — *Darren*

"Cherish the time you spend with your family, and never take anything for granted." — *Juli*

Darren Woodson with DJ - after a long day at Disneyland (May, 1997)

What I Value Most

"We both value our children the most." — *Darren and Juli*

Favorite Pre-Game or Post-Game Meal

Post-Game - "Juli's tacos." — *Darren*

BORN

Darren - 4-25-69

Juli - 5-22-70

COLLEGE

Darren - Arizona State

Juli - North Texas

YEARS IN NFL

6th Year

Dallas Cowboys

SPOUSE'S OCCUPATION

Wife & mother

ANNIVERSARY

May 6 - 2 years

10 years together

CHILDREN

DJ - 5 years

Miranda - 1 year

PETS

Saiko - Akita

My Last Meal Would Be

"Smothered pork chops, greens, mashed potatoes, yams, and apple pie." *—Darren*

"Filet mignon covered with A.1., baked potato with everything, and anything chocolate!" *—Juli*

The Woodsons - Darren, Juli (holding Miranda), and DJ - enjoying the off-season together in Phoenix, Arizona

Favorite Childhood Snack

"Peanut butter and jelly sandwich." *—Darren*

"Ravioli, and grilled cheese sandwich." *—Juli*

Favorite Holiday or Holiday Tradition

"Christmas." *—Darren and Juli*

Favorite City outside of Dallas

"Phoenix, Arizona." —*Darren and Juli*

Hobbies and Other Interests

"Reading, listening to music, and spending time with my wife and kids." —*Darren*

"Family time, decorating my home, and traveling." —*Juli*

Most Memorable Moment in Life outside of Pro-Football

"Getting married." —*Darren*

"Getting married, and having my two children." —*Juli*

Favorite Time of Day and Why

"11 p.m. - go to sleep!" —*Darren*

"Evening - quality time with Darren and kids." —*Juli*

Juli and Miranda - at Miranda's first birthday party in Phoenix, Arizona (May, 1997)

Lemon Poppy Seed Cake

- 1 package Lemon Cake Mix
- 1¼ cups water
- 3 egg whites
- 3 tablespoons poppy seed
- ⅓ cup oil

GLAZE

- 1 cup confectioners' sugar
- 3 to 4 teaspoons lemon juice

Heat oven to 350 degrees. Grease and flour a 12-cup Bundt pan. Empty cake mix into a large bowl; add water, egg whites, poppy seed, and oil. Mix well. Bake, and cool. For glaze: Combine sugar and lemon juice; stir, until well-blended. Drizzle over the top of cake. One Bundt cake makes 16 servings.

Spicy Catfish

- ½ teaspoon oil
- 1 cup onion, thinly-sliced
- 1 pound boneless catfish
- ½ teaspoon pepper
- ½ teaspoon garlic powder
- 2 medium tomatoes, chopped
- Tabasco sauce

Heat oven to 425 degrees. Coat 13" x 9" x 2" baking pan lightly with oil. Layer half of the onions in bottom of the pan. Place fish on top of onions. Sprinkle with pepper and garlic powder. Cover with chopped tomatoes and remaining onion slices. Dot top onions with Tabasco sauce. Bake at 425 degrees for 20 to 25 minutes, or until fish flakes easily with fork. Makes 4 servings.

Coaches and Staff

Hubbard "Axe" & Gloria Alexander

Assistant Coach
Wide Receivers

Philosophy to Live by

"Be true to yourself." — *Axe*
"Honesty and truthfulness to self and others." — *Gloria*

Hubbard "Axe" Alexander - became the wide receivers' coach for the Cowboys in 1989

Best Advice I Could Give to a High School Senior

"Be dedicated." — *Axe*

"Understand these are great years, and do your best to build a strong foundation." — *Gloria*

What I Value Most

"My family." — *Axe*

"My integrity." — *Gloria*

Best Asset

"Honesty, caring, and giving of myself." — *Axe*

"Concern for others." — *Gloria*

BORN

Axe - 2-14-39

Gloria - 9-9

COLLEGE

Axe - Tennessee State

Gloria - Tennessee State & Memphis

YEARS IN NFL

8 Years

Dallas Cowboys

SPOUSE'S OCCUPATION

Classroom instructor

ANNIVERSARY

May 27 - 35 years

CHILDREN

Todd - 32 years

Chad - 22 years

Bard - 17 years

PETS

Simba - Cocker Spaniel

Biggest Challenge Ever Faced in Life

"As a high school student - dealing with the deaths of my mother, father, and brother." — *Axe*

"Facing the fact that I had no choice but to drive the car if I were to work, after being driven for fifteen years." — *Gloria*

If I Were Not in Professional Football I Would Be

"High school principal." — *Axe*

Three People I Would Invite to a "Fantasy" Dinner Party

"Michael Jordan, Tiger Woods, and Maxwell." — *Axe*

Former Cowboys Player/Coach Most Admired and Why

"Charles Haley - brutally honest." — *Axe*

"Russell Maryland - intelligent, hardworking, and spiritual individual." — *Gloria*

Game Day Rituals

"Early workout, team breakfast meeting, return home, and drive to stadium with my son." — *Axe*

"Give no thoughts to the game - find a ride, select wardrobe - all to procrastinate." — *Gloria*

Favorite Pre-Game or Post-Game Meal

"Pancakes." — *Axe*

My Last Meal Would Be

"Seafood Gumbo." — *Axe*

"Whatever I could select from Luby's Cafeteria." — *Gloria*

Favorite Childhood Snack

"Peanut butter with jelly sandwich." — *Axe*

"Hostess cupcakes with a glass of milk." — *Gloria*

Favorite Holiday or Holiday Tradition

"Christmas - giving." — *Axe*

"Decorating home for Christmas." — *Gloria*

Favorite City outside of Dallas

"Chicago, Illinois." — *Axe*

"Nashville, Tennessee." — *Gloria*

Hobbies and Other Interests

"Power distance walking." — *Axe*

"Collecting African-American art." — *Gloria*

Most Memorable Moment in Life outside of Pro-Football

"National Championships in college football." — *Axe*

"Gaining true friends in the six cities in which we have lived." — *Gloria*

Favorite Time of Day and Why

"5:00 a.m. - all around me are asleep." — *Axe*

"Whenever I am alone during the day." — *Gloria*

Buttermilk Baked Chicken

1 frying chicken (3-pound), cut in parts
2 cups buttermilk
¾ cup flour
1½ teaspoon salt
¼ teaspoon pepper
¼ cup butter
1 can (10¾-ounce) cream of chicken soup

Mix flour, salt, and pepper. Dip chicken pieces in ½ cup buttermilk; roll in the seasoned flour. Put butter in a 13" x 9" x 2" baking pan; melt in a 425-degree oven. Put chicken in pan (skin side down); bake for 30 minutes. Turn; bake for 15 minutes longer. Mix remaining buttermilk with the soup; pour around chicken. Bake 15 minutes longer, or until tender.

* This makes a delicious gravy to be put over rice or potatoes.

Joe Avezzano - doing one of his favorite things

If I Were Not in Professional Football I Would Be

"In the entertainment industry." —*Joe*

Favorite Time of Day and Why

"Night - places are rockin'." —*Joe*

"Twilight - it's peaceful and still." —*Diann*

Joe, Tony, and Diann Avezzano

Most Memorable Moment in Life outside of Pro-Football

"Marriage, and birth of Tony." —*Joe*

"My wedding to Joe." —*Diann*

Joseph W. "Joe" & Diann Avezzano

Assistant Coach
Special Teams

Best Advice I Could Give to a High School Senior

""Strap yourself in, hang on tight, get your mind right, and enjoy the ride." — *Joe*

"Enjoy life and people, and work hard." — *Diann*

Celebrating Tony's 21st birthday - left to right: Candice, our son's friend; Tony; Joe; and Diann

Philosophy to Live by

"Don't ever lose the excitement and enjoyment of learning, living, loving, and expanding oneself." —*Joe*

"Do unto others as you would have them do unto you." —*Diann*

Three People I Would Invite to a "Fantasy" Dinner Party

"John F. Kennedy, Martin Luther King, and Merle Haggard." —*Joe*

BORN

Joe - 11-17-43

Diann - 3-10-49

COLLEGE

Joe - Florida State

Diann - Patricia Stevens Fashion Merchandising

YEARS IN NFL

8th Year

Dallas Cowboys

SPOUSE'S OCCUPATION

Small business owner / fashion jewelry

ANNIVERSARY

June 17- 23 years

CHILDREN

Tony - 21 years

PETS

Butterscotch - Cat

Former Cowboys Player/Coach Most Admired and Why

"Tony Dorsett - have watched him grow on/off field since he was in high school. I like what I saw and see." —*Joe*

Game Day Rituals

"Enjoy the moment—very special moments every week." —*Joe*

"Get nervous, and don't talk too much." —*Diann*

My Last Meal Would Be

"Pasta." —*Joe*

"Sushi." —*Diann*

Favorite Childhood Snack

"Chocolate chip cookies." —*Joe*

"Cinnamon toast." —*Diann*

Hobbies and Other Interests

"Music, and planning and being part of projects other people can enjoy." —*Joe*

"Cooking, and reading." —*Diann*

Olive Oil & Balsamic Bread Dip

- 1 cup extra virgin olive oil
- ⅓ cup balsamic vinegar
- 1 teaspoon granulated garlic
- ½ teaspoon coursely-ground black pepper
- ½ teaspoon sweet basil
- 1 teaspoon oregano

On plate, or in shallow bowl, pour the oil & vinegar together; sprinkle with garlic, pepper, basil and oregano. Stir, and serve with any good fresh bread. Just dip the bread in it.

James "Jim" & Beverly Bates

Assistant Coach
Linebackers

Beverly & Jim Bates

BORN

Jim - 5-31-46

Beverly - 9-4-46

COLLEGE

Jim - Tennessee

Beverly - UCLA

YEARS IN NFL

7th Year

Dallas Cowboys (2)

Atlanta Falcons (1)

Cleveland Browns (4)

SPOUSE'S OCCUPATION

Fashion coordinator

CHILDREN

James, Jr. - 24 years

Jeremy - 20 years

Favorite Holiday or Holiday Tradition

"Christmas Eve and Christmas Day." — *Beverly*

Gazpacho

3 cups tomato juice
dash of red pepper sauce
2 tablespoons vegetable oil
1 tablespoon white wine vinegar
1 or 2 cucumbers, peeled, seeded, and minced
1 green pepper, seeded and finely-chopped
1 clove garlic, pressed
½ cup cold water
1 small onion, finely-minced

In a blender or food processor, blend together the tomato juice, red pepper sauce, vinegar, and oil. Add pressed garlic, cucumbers, green pepper, onions, and cold water. Combine all ingredients well. Chill, covered, for at least one hour before serving.

Jim; James and Jeremy (sons); Beverly (left); and Tina

Charlie & Stephanie Biggurs

Assistant Strength & Conditioning

Philosophy to Live by

"Trust in God and lean not unto your own understanding." — *Charlie*

"Be anxious for nothing, but in everything by prayer and supplication, with thanksgiving, let your requests be made known to God." — *Stephanie*

Stephanie and Charlie Biggurs

Best Advice I Could Give to a High School Senior

"Be disciplined." — *Charlie*

"Stay focused on one goal at a time. High school does pay off." — *Stephanie*

What I Value Most

"My relationship with Jesus Christ, and my marriage." — *Charlie*

"My relationship with God, and my family." — *Stephanie*

BORN

Charlie - 6-13-69

COLLEGE

Charlie - Texas Tech

Stephanie - Texas Tech

YEARS IN NFL

1st Year

Dallas Cowboys

SPOUSE'S OCCUPATION

Receptionist for Dallas Cowboys

ANNIVERSARY

March 11 - 2 years

CHILDREN

Christopher - 1 year

Best Asset

"My wife, and my Bible." — *Charlie*

"My husband, and my Bible." — *Stephanie*

Biggest Challenge Ever Faced in Life

"College." — *Charlie*

"Having a baby." — *Stephanie*

If I Were Not in Professional Football I Would Be

"In high school sports." — *Charlie*

Charlie - with son, Chistopher

Two People I Would Invite to a "Fantasy" Dinner Party

"Bishop T. D. Jakes and Nelson Mandela." — *Charlie*

Former Cowboys Player/Coach Most Admired and Why

"Roger Staubach." — *Charlie*

Favorite Pre-Game or Post-Game Meal

"Pasta." — *Charlie*

My Last Meal Would Be

"Catfish and fries." — *Charlie*

Zesty Meatloaf

2 pounds ground beef
1 large green pepper
1 large onion
2 green onions
1 egg
1 teaspoon garlic
1 teaspoon seasoned salt
½ teaspoon red pepper
2 tablespoons flour
1 can diced tomatoes, or 1 large, fresh tomato
1 package Lawry's chicken-teriyaki marinade

SAUCE

1 can fiesta nacho cheese sauce
1 can cream of mushroom soup (plain or golden)
1 tablespoon Dijon mustard

Cut up vegetables. Mix all ingredients together. Shape into a mold; bake at 350 degrees for 30 to 45 minutes.

For sauce, mix all ingredients together; heat. You can either pour over the entire meatloaf, and bake for another 10 minutes, or you can pour over individual slices.

Most Memorable Moment in Life outside of Pro-Football

"The day I got married to my wonderful wife." — *Charlie*

"The day my son entered the world." — *Stephanie*

Favorite Time of Day and Why

"Evening - I like to watch the sunset." — *Charlie*

"Early morning - it's quiet, peaceful, and everything is still moving slow." — *Stephanie*

Crab Cakes Maryland

2 tablespoons chopped fresh parsley
1 teaspoon dry mustard
1 teaspoon Worcestershire, or dash of Tabasco
2 eggs, beaten
2 tablespoons mayonnaise
1 pound cooked crab, flaked or broken up
1 cup fresh bread crumbs, or ½ cup unsalted cracker crumbs
salt and pepper, to taste
flour, for dredging

Mix the parsley, dry mustard, Worcestershire or Tabasco, eggs, and mayonnaise together. Add the crab and crumbs; season with salt and pepper, to taste. Divide the mixture into 8 cakes; dredge in flour. Deep-fry at 375 to 380-degrees for 2 to 3 minutes, or until golden brown (you may pan-fry them on both sides in a bit of butter). Serve with a big salad. Makes 4 servings.

Joe's Florida Stone Crab Mustard Sauce

*Joe's Stone Crab Restaurant in Miami Beach

3½ teaspoons dry English mustard (Colman's)
1 cup mayonnaise
2 teaspoons Worcestershire sauce
1 teaspoon A.1. sauce
½ cup light cream or half-and-half
½ teaspoon salt

Mix together all ingredients. Keep refrigerated, when not using.

Robert G. & Diana Blackwell

Video Director

Philosophy to Live by

"Always make decisions because they are what you want, not what you think others want of you." — *Robert*

"Set your goals high and keep them; if you fail, pick yourself up and try again." — *Diana*

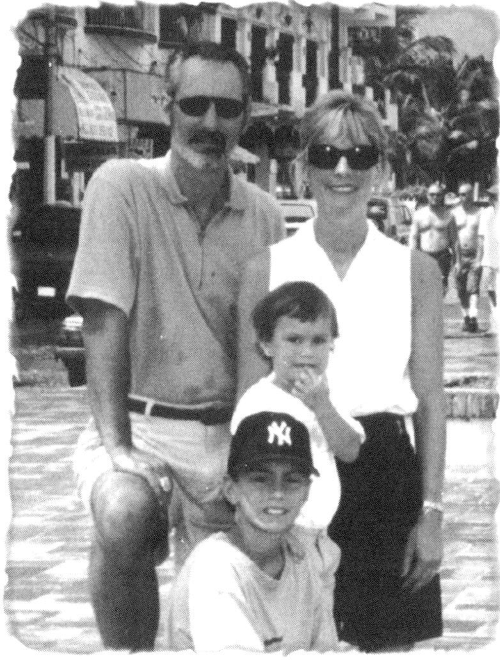

The whole Blackwell family - on vacation (June, 1997) in Puerto Vallarta, Mexico, on the Boardwalk - top to bottom: Robert, Diana, Lora, and Nate

Best Advice I Could Give to a High School Senior

"The choices you will make today will effect the rest of your life, so choose carefully."
— *Robert*

"Stay on the right track!" — *Diana*

BORN

Robert - 12-1-50

Diana - 5-25-58

COLLEGE

Robert - Stephen F. Austin

Diana - California Lutheran

YEARS IN NFL

17th Year

Dallas Cowboys

SPOUSE'S OCCUPATION

Flight attendant for American Airlines

ANNIVERSARY

March 16 - 12 years

CHILDREN

Nathaniel "Nathan" - 9 years

Lora Ann - 3 years

PETS

Lady Blackwell - 5-year-old Sheltie

What I Value Most

"Marriage, family, and religion." — *Robert*

"Family, friends, religion, and health." — *Diana*

Robert and Diana - on the town in New York City's All Star Cafe (April, 1997)

Best Asset

"Patience." — *Robert*

"Being friendly to others." — *Diana*

Biggest Challenge Ever Faced in Life

"Fatherhood." — *Robert*

"Parenthood, and all of life's challenges." — *Diana*

If I Were Not in Professional Football I Would Be

"Documentary film maker." — *Robert*

Three People I Would Invite to a "Fantasy" Dinner Party

"Moses, Ansel Adams, and Robert Duvall." — *Robert*

Game Day Rituals

"Always wear my lucky shirt." — *Robert*

"Bringing friends with me to the game." — *Diana*

My Last Meal Would Be

"Sautéed scallops and blackened red fish." — *Robert*

"Poached salmon from Yvette's in Dallas." — *Diana*

Hobbies and Other Interests

"Helping coach youth baseball." — *Robert*

"Being involved with kids' school activities, PTO, Coppell Investment Club #2, and Coppell Womens Club." — *Diana*

Craig W. Boller

Assistant Coach
Defensive Tackles

Best Advice I Could Give to a High School Senior

"There are many setbacks in life - how you deal with each will determine your success and quality of life." — *Craig*

Craig Boller, with daughter,
Kimberly Stadler - at June 21st wedding

Philosophy to Live by

"Live each day to the fullest - it could be your last." — *Craig*

What I Value Most

"My family." — *Craig*

Best Asset

"Wit." — *Craig*

Biggest Challenge Ever Faced in Life

"Loss of job." — *Craig*

If I Were Not in Professional Football I Would Be

"Education." — *Craig*

BORN

1-29-48

COLLEGE

Iowa State

YEARS IN NFL

2nd Year

Dallas Cowboys

CHILDREN

Valerie Juul - 29 years

Kimberly Stadler - 26 years

GRANDCHILDREN

MacKenzie Juul - newborn

Craig's daughters: Valerie Juul; and Kimberly Stadler (white top)

Three People I Would Invite to a "Fantasy" Dinner Party

Bill Murray, Goldie Hawn, and Jack Nicholson." — *Craig*

Former Cowboys Player/Coach Most Admired and Why

Bob Lilly - physical and mental skills." — *Craig*

Favorite Pre-Game or Post-Game Meal

"Pasta." — *Craig*

My Last Meal Would Be

"Butterfly chop, veggies, and Uncle Ben's Original Rice Recipe." — *Craig*

Favorite Childhood Snack

"Peanut butter, or Oreo cookies." — *Craig*

Favorite Holiday or Holiday Tradition

"Christmas - family gathering." — *Craig*

"Grandpa" Boller, with MacKenzie Juul (6 months)

Favorite City outside of Dallas

"Austin, Texas." — *Craig*

Hobbies and Other Interests

"Boating, fishing, and golf." — *Craig*

Most Memorable Moment in Life outside of Pro-Football

"Birth of my daughter, Valerie." — *Craig*

Favorite Time of Day and Why

"Early morning - peace and quiet." — *Craig*

Mexican Lasagna

- 1 pound lean ground beef
- 1 can (16-ounce) refried beans
- 2 teaspoons dried oregano
- 1 teaspoon ground cumin
- ¾ teaspoon garlic powder
- 12 uncooked lasagna noodles
- 2½ cups water
- 2½ cups picante sauce or salsa
- 2 cups sour cream
- ¾ cup finely-sliced green onions
- 1 can (2.2 ounces) sliced black olives, drained
- 1 cup shredded Monterey Jack cheese

Combine beef, beans, oregano, cumin, and garlic powder together. Place four of the uncooked lasagna noodles in the bottom of a 13" x 9" x 2" baking pan. Spread half of the beef mixture over the noodles. Top with four more noodles and the remaining beef mixture. Cover with the remaining noodles. Combine water and picante sauce; pour over all. Cover tightly with foil; bake at 350 degrees for 1½ hours, or until noodles are tender. Combine sour cream, onions, and olives; spoon over casserole and top with cheese. Bake, uncovered, until cheese is melted (about 5 minutes) Makes 12 servings.

Brodsky family picture

Jeff Brodsky's Hot (No-Fry) Crispy Wings

10 whole chicken wings (feeds 2 to 4 as appetizer)
1 cup flour
Louisiana Hot Sauce
oil
salt
pepper

Preheat oven to 425 to 450 degrees. Combine flour, salt, and pepper in bag. Cut wings in half. Place in bag; shake well. Use broil pan (*comes with oven - 12" x 14"*). Cover bottom of pan with oil, or use spray oil; place chicken pieces, skin down; space evenly. Bake for 30 minutes; turn, and bake for 30 minutes more, or until brown. Remove; cover with hot sauce. Serve immediately.

*Can serve with Bleu Cheese Dressing and celery pieces

Joe & Joyce Brodsky

Assistant Coach
Running Backs

Philosophy to Live by

"Derive pleasure each day from doing for others." — *Joe*

"Yesterday is history; tomorrow is a mystery; today is a gift - that's why they say it's the present." — *Joyce*

Joyce and Joe Brodsky

Best Advice I Could Give to a High School Senior

"Set your goals high; strive to be the best; arriving takes care of itself." —*Joe*

"You are unique - very important with special gifts; you should work as hard as you can to develop the gifts God has given to you." —*Joyce*

What I Value Most

"Family and friends." —*Joe*

"Family, friends, and health." —*Joyce*

BORN

Joe - 6-9-34

COLLEGE

Joe - Florida

Joyce - Miami (FL)

YEARS IN NFL

9th Year

Dallas Cowboys

SPOUSE'S OCCUPATION

Retired schoolteacher / Travel agent - Journey's Abroad

ANNIVERSARY

August 17 - 40 years

CHILDREN

Joe, Jr. - 39 years (wife: Robin)

Larry - 37 years

Jeff - 35 years (wife: Frances)

GRANDCHILDREN

Amanda - 10 years

Joey - 7 years

Nina - 1 year

Best Asset

"Compassion for others, and ability to work with people." —*Joe*

"Positive attitude." —*Joyce*

Biggest Challenge Ever Faced in Life

"Taking on responsibility of family and life." —*Joe*

"Balancing three boys, husband, and career." —*Joyce*

Brodsky family picture

Three People I Would Invite to a "Fantasy" Dinner Party

"Paul Newman, Sophia Loren, and General Schwartzkoff." —*Joe*

Former Cowboys Player/Coach Most Admired and Why

"Tex Schramm - he's the original reason the Cowboys are America's Team." —*Joe*

"Roger Staubach - character, values, family man, and serves community." —*Joyce*

Game Day Rituals

"Ride to stadium with Coach Avezzano, visit the wheelchair-bound fans, and kiss all the ladies when we win." —*Joe*

"Not sleeping well the night before; watching/listening to all TV analysts and Cowboys' TV shows; wearing Super Bowl jewelry for luck; and picking up Diann Avezzano." —*Joyce*

My Last Meal Would Be

"Free." —*Joe*

"Rack of lamb and rice pilaf." —*Joyce*

Britt & Laura Brown

Assistant Trainer

Philosophy to Live by

"Always try to make the best of everything." — *Britt*

"Don't get impatient or upset about daily petty things; enjoy life." — *Laura*

Chase and Sydney Brown

Best Advice I Could Give to a High School Senior

"Find something that you have an interest in and spend your time involved in it." — *Britt*

What I Value Most

"Family." — *Britt*

"God, and my family." — *Laura*

Biggest Challenge Ever Faced in Life

"Coaching change in Miami in 1996." — *Britt*

"Moving to Miami." — *Laura*

If I Were Not in Professional Football I Would Be

"In the college setting." — *Britt*

BORN

Britt - 7-6-64

Laura - 6-7-67

COLLEGE

Britt - TCU

Laura - TCU

YEARS IN NFL

6th Year

Dallas Cowboys (2)

Intern Year with Cowboys (1)

Miami Dolphins (4)

SPOUSE'S OCCUPATION

Medical Transcriptionist / Homemaker

ANNIVERSARY

December 9 - 7 years

CHILDREN

Chase - 3 years

Sydney - 1 year

PETS

Tex - Turtle

Three People I Would Invite to a "Fantasy" Dinner Party

"Arnold Schwarzenegger, Regis Philbin, and Elizabeth Vargas." — *Britt*

Britt, Sydney, Chase, and Laura - visiting grandparents in the hill country

Former Cowboys Player/Coach Most Admired and Why

"Randy White - always gave all he had at everything." — *Britt*

My Last Meal Would Be

"Rib-eye steak (big), and homemade ice cream." — *Britt*

"Fried seafood platter with loaded baked potato." — *Laura*

Favorite Childhood Snack

"Popcorn." — *Britt*

"Bread with sugar sprinkled on the top." — *Laura*

Most Memorable Moment in Life outside of Pro-Football

"My wife having both of our children." — *Britt*

"Our wedding, and the birth of Chase and Sydney." — *Laura*

Favorite Time of Day and Why

"After practice - it's over and, hopefully, we have no new injuries." — *Britt*

"Early morning - because the house is quiet and peaceful when everyone is still asleep." — *Laura*

Pasta and Sausage Dish

2 cups tri-color penne rigate mostaccioli
1 pound Ekridge sausage, cut in thin slices
1 can sliced black olives
1 cup broccoli florets
½ cup onion, chopped
½ cup pine nuts
¾ cup sun-dried tomatoes
olive oil (or other type oil)
salt and pepper, to taste

Cook pasta, according to package directions. Sauté onion in oil; add broccoli. Simmer, until broccoli is desired firmness. Add all other ingredients; simmer until warm.

Britt's Mom's Chicken Spaghetti

1 large chicken, boiled and boned (keep broth)
1 package (12-ounce) spaghetti
½ pound grated cheese
1 can cream of mushroom soup
1 small jar mushrooms
1 can tomatoes
1 cup bell pepper, chopped
1 cup onion, chopped
1 cup celery, chopped
2 tablespoons Worcestershire sauce
juice of 1 lemon
1 tablespoon sugar
salt and pepper, to taste

Sauté onions, celery, and bell pepper in 4 tablespoons of chicken broth; simmer. Then, add other ingredients (except for spaghetti, cheese, and mushrooms). Bring remaining broth to a boil, (adding water, if necessary), to cook spaghetti; drain. Add to chicken mixture. Place in casserole dish; add sliced mushrooms on top. Bake at 350 degrees for 20 minutes. Add cheese; bake for 10 more minutes.

* Excellent with smoked turkey (substituting for chicken). To freeze: do not add cheese. . .and do not cook!

Santa Fe Chicken

1¼ pounds chicken breasts, boned and skinned
1 teaspoon paprika
1 teaspoon salt
¼ teaspoon pepper
1 tablespoon cooking oil
1 small green pepper, chopped
1 medium onion, chopped
1 clove garlic, chopped (or garlic powder equal to 1 clove)
1 can Ro-Tel tomatoes
1½ cups chicken broth
1½ cups Minute Rice
¾ cup shredded Cheddar or Monterey Jack cheese

Cut chicken into thin strips; sprinkle with paprika, salt, and pepper. In 10-inch skillet, heat oil, over medium-high heat. Cook chicken in oil for 2 minutes. Add onion, green pepper, and garlic; cook, until tender (about 4 minutes), stirring frequently. Add Ro-Tel tomatoes and the chicken broth; bring to a boil. Stir in the rice. Remove from heat, and cover; let stand about 5 minutes, or until all liquid is absorbed. Sprinkle with the cheese, and serve. Makes 4 servings.

Pineapple Cake

CAKE
1 yellow cake mix
4 eggs
1 cup oil
1 can mandarin oranges (do not drain)

FROSTING
1 container (9-ounce) of Cool Whip
1 can (15-ounce) crushed pineapple (do not drain)
1 small package of vanilla instant pudding.

Mix all together; put in a greased and floured pan. Bake at 350 degrees for about 30 minutes. Let cake cool.

To make the frosting: Mix all ingredients together; put on top of cake.

William A. "Bucky" & Amy Buchanan

Philosophy to Live by

"Honesty." — *Bucky*

"Be true to yourself and your dreams - never give up!" — *Amy*

Assistant Equipment Manager

BORN

Bucky - 6-9-61

Amy - 4-3-65

YEARS IN NFL

4th Year

Dallas Cowboys

SPOUSE'S OCCUPATION

Administrative Asst - EDS

ANNIVERSARY

May 25 -12 years

CHILDREN

William "Thomas", II - 11 years

Jonathan "Brett" - 8 years

PETS

Barney - Cocker Spaniel

Bucky and Amy Buchanan - sightseeing in Las Vegas

What I Value Most

"My wife, Amy, and sons, Thomas and Brett." — *Bucky*

Best Asset

"Parents who cared." — *Bucky*

"Strong family ties, and my faith." — Amy

Biggest Challenge Ever Faced in Life

"Living with my wife." — *Bucky*

"He loves a good challenge." *(Amy's Reply)*

Former Cowboys Player/Coach Most Admired and Why

"Randy White - for the way he played each game." — *Bucky*

Thomas and Brett - first day of school ('96-'97)

My Last Meal Would Be

"Steak and potatoes." — *Bucky*

"Steak, mushrooms, and lobster." — *Amy*

Favorite Childhood Snack

"Mom's Lemon Chess Pie." — *Bucky*

"Dad's butter and sugar sandwiches." — *Amy*

Favorite Holiday or Holiday Tradition

"Christmas - just being with family." — *Bucky*

"Fourth of July - homemade ice cream, and watching fireworks with the children." — *Amy*

Favorite City outside of Dallas

"Washington, D. C."— *Bucky*

"Maui, Hawaii." — *Amy*

Hobbies and Other Interests

"Golf, yard work, and playing ball with the boys." — *Bucky*

"Reading, martial arts, and spending time with family and good friends." — *Amy*

Most Memorable Moment in Life outside of Pro-Football

"The birth of my two sons." — *Bucky*

"Ditto - and breaking my first board in martial arts." — *Amy*

David "Dave" & Kay Campo

Assistant Coach
Defensive
Coordinator

Philosophy to Live by

"Use what God has given you to be the best that you can be." — *Dave*

Dave and Kay Campo - at Christmas

Born

Dave - 7-18-47

Kay - 7-22-56

College

Dave - Central Connecticut State

Kay - Stevens Henniger Business College

Years in NFL

9th Year

Dallas Cowboys

Spouse's Occupation

Homemaker

Children

Angie - 22 years

Eric - 21 years

Shelbie - 17 years

Michael - 6 years

Dave has two children from previous marriage:

Becky - 20 years

Tommy - 18 years

Best Advice I Could Give to a High School Senior

"The only limitations you have are those you put on yourself." — *Dave*

What I Value Most

"Children." — *Dave*

"Family." — *Kay*

Best Asset

"Ability to deal with different kinds of people." — *Dave*

Campo's son, Eric, with daughter, Madyson - 1½ years

Biggest Challenge Ever Faced in Life

"Raising children." —*Dave and Kay*

If I Were Not in Professional Football I Would Be

"An actor (musical comedy) or singer." —*Dave*

Former Cowboys Player/Coach Most Admired and Why

"Roger Staubach - smart, competitive, leader, winner, and good Christian." —*Dave*

My Last Meal Would Be

"My grandmother's northern Italian spaghetti." —*Dave*

"Baby back ribs." — *Kay*

Favorite Childhood Snack

"Peach pie." —*Dave*

"Homemade bread and jam." — *Kay*

Favorite City outside of Dallas

"Mystic, Connecticut." —*Dave*

Hobbies and Other Interests

"Listening and dancing to oldies (jitterbug), playing guitar (folk music), and son's T-ball games." —*Dave*

"Scrapbooks, crafts, reading, and children's sports and activities." — *Kay*

Favorite Time of Day and Why

"All day." —*Dave*

"Evening - because we can spend time together as a family." — *Kay*

Baby Back Ribs

3 pounds pork baby back ribs, cut apart
1 cup brown sugar
½ cup soy sauce
½ cup ketchup

Place ribs, fatty side down, in baking dish; cover. Bake at 450 degrees for 30 minutes; drain juice. Brush ribs with sauce; turn over, and brush with sauce. Cover; bake another 30 minutes at 350 degrees. Drain; brush ribs again. Bake, uncovered, another 15 minutes.

Sauce:

Bring sugar, soy sauce, and ketchup to a slow boil, over low heat, while stirring. Remove from heat.

Campo children: Angie, Michael, and Shelbie

Chicken Marinade

½ cup white vinegar
⅓ cup oil
½ teaspoon Worcestershire sauce
5 drops Tabasco sauce
½ tablespoon ketchup
1 teaspoon paprika
3 chopped green onions
1 clove garlic, crushed
3 teaspoons salt
½ teaspoon dry mustard

Mix all ingredients together. Pour into zip-loc bag with chicken. Marinate 12 to 24 hours.

Rustic Potato Wedges

4 russet potatoes
1 tablespoon vegetable oil
¼ teaspoon pepper
⅛ teaspoon salt
2 cloves garlic

Cut potatoes into large wedges, keeping skin on. Put into bowl of cold water; let stand 15 minutes (to remove fat). Heat oven to 425 degrees. Spray non-stick baking sheet with cooking spray. Drain potatoes. Mix ingredients; toss with potatoes. Arrange on baking sheet. Bake for 20 minutes. Use spatula to turn. Bake for 20 more minutes.

Rich & Ros Dalrymple

Director of Public Relations

Philosophy to Live by

"Do unto others as you would have them do unto you." — *Ros*

Rich, Clay, and Kim - canoeing in Daingerfield State Park in East Texas

Best Advice I Could Give to a High School Senior

"Keep one eye on where you are and one eye on where you want to be." — *Rich*

"Tell the truth - lying is always worse." — *Ros*

What I Value Most

"My wife, children, and our happiness." — *Rich*

"Family, health, and friends." — *Ros*

BORN

Rich - 8-2-60

Ros - 1-10-64

COLLEGE

Rich - Westminster College - Pennsylvania

Ros - Miami (FL)

YEARS IN NFL

8th Year

Dallas Cowboys

SPOUSE'S OCCUPATION

Homemaker

ANNIVERSARY

July 9 - 9 years

CHILDREN

Kimberley - 6 years

Clayton - 4 years

Best Asset

"Enjoy people." — *Rich*

"Automatic coffee maker, and dishwasher (children, of course)." — *Ros*

Biggest Challenge Ever Faced in Life

"Overcoming the loss of my father." — *Rich*

"Graduating from college, finding a job, and getting a life going." — *Ros*

Three People We Would Invite to a "Fantasy" Dinner Party

"Princess Diana, John Madden, and Joe Namath." — *Rich and Ros*

Former Cowboys Player/Coach Most Admired and Why

"Roger Staubach - for his success away from the game of football." — *Rich*

"Norv Turner - for his wife, Nancy." — *Ros*

Game Day Rituals

"Visit the Madden cruiser, prior to Fox broadcasts, with John Madden and Pat Summerall." — *Rich*

"Stay home, invite friends over, cook during pre-game, and eat the whole game long." — *Ros*

My Last Meal Would Be

"A steak at Del Frisco's." — *Rich*

"Beer, bread, and gourmet salads." — *Ros*

Favorite Holiday or Holiday Tradition

"Thanksgiving dinner on the Friday following a Cowboys' victory." — *Rich*

"Safaris, or beaches." — *Ros*

Most Memorable Moment in Life outside of Pro-Football

"Having kids, and playing on an undefeated college football team." — *Rich*

"Winning a match at Wimbeldon, and having children." — *Ros*

Robert L. & Janice Ford

Assistant Coach
Tight Ends

Philosophy to Live by

"Treat others the way you want to be treated." — *Robert*

"Be true to yourself, and be the best person that you can be." — *Janice*

The Fords - Bobby, Janice, Robert, and Jason - in their Cowboys' duds!

Best Advice I Could Give to a High School Senior

"Be prepared to study harder." — *Robert*

"Stay at home as long as you can, because it is a big, bad world out there." — *Janice*

What I Value Most

"My family." — *Robert*

"Robert, Bobby, and Jason." — *Janice*

Best Asset

"Perseverance." — *Robert*

"My ability to assess other people." — *Janice*

BORN

Robert - 6-21-51

Janice - 4-8-54

COLLEGE

Robert - Houston & Western Illinois

Janice - Delta College & American Institute of Banking

YEARS IN NFL

7th Year

Dallas Cowboys

SPOUSE'S OCCUPATION

Wife, mother, & Robert's biggest fan

ANNIVERSARY

April 26 - 22 years

CHILDREN

Bobby - 21 years

Jason - 19 years

Biggest Challenge Ever Faced in Life

"Growing up." — *Robert*

"Becoming a parent." —*Janice*

Four People I Would Invite to a "Fantasy" Dinner Party

"Bill Cosby, Jimmy Stewart, Raymond Burr, and President John F. Kennedy." — *Robert*

Former Cowboys Player/Coach Most Admired and Why

"Robert Newhouse - because of who he is and why." — *Robert*

"Roger Staubach - values and his success." —*Janice*

Game Day Rituals

"Rise very early, have breakfast, and wake Janice - so she can help me get dressed." — *Robert*

"Not getting much sleep the night before, and helping Robert get dressed." —*Janice*

My Last Meal Would Be

"Piece of watermelon." — *Robert*

"Alaskan King Crab legs." —*Janice*

Favorite Childhood Snack

"Salami sandwich." — *Robert*

"My mom's bread pudding." —*Janice*

Most Memorable Moment in Life outside of Pro-Football

"The day Janice and I got married, and the births of my boys." — *Robert*

"My wedding day, and the days I had my sons." —*Janice*

Favorite Time of Day and Why

"Early morning - the freshness of the air and the look of the sky." — *Robert*

"Late night - because it's quiet and I can read a book without being bothered." —*Janice*

Our Friend Fran's Flank Steak Marinade

2 tablespoons garlic powder
2 tablespoons onion powder (not salt)
¾ cup vegetable oil (Wesson or Crisco)
¼ cup soy sauce
¼ to ½ cup honey (depends on taste)
3 tablespoons red wine vinegar
1 tablespoon Worcestershire sauce

Mix ingredients together (2 or more hours before grilling).
Pour over steak; refrigerate in a covered dish, turning occasionally — *the longer, the better. Fire up grill (medium hot to hot grill). Cook 4 to 5 minutes per side (for rare to medium), and 6 to 7 minutes per side (for medium to well-done).*

Corn Pudding

3 eggs, slightly-beaten
1 can (15-ounce) cream-style corn
1 can (15-ounce) whole kernel corn (do not drain)
1 box Jiffy Corn Muffin Mix
½ stick butter, melted
salt and pepper, to taste
Optional: ¼ cup finely-chopped green onions or bell pepper *(this ingredient will rise to the top; adds color)*

Mix all ingredients together well. Preheat oven to 350 degrees. Spray casserole dish with Pam spray. Pour mixture into casserole dish. Bake for one hour.
*A vegetable dish — *not to be confused with dessert.*

Chicken Teriyaki

⅔ cup soy sauce
¼ cup white wine
2 tablespoons sugar
1 clove garlic, minced
1 tablespoon salad oil
½ teaspoon ground ginger
1 medium-size fryer, cut-up

Combine soy sauce, wine, sugar, garlic, salad oil, and ginger. Marinate chicken in this mixture for at least 1 hour, or overnight. Grill on outdoor grill, or bake at 325 degrees. Baste several times while cooking. Makes 4 servings.

Biggest Challenge Ever Faced in Life

"Obtaining my college degree." — *Emily*

If I Were Not in Professional Football I Would Be

"Year-round 4-H camp director." — *Bob*

Three People I Would Invite to a "Fantasy" Dinner Party

"Cal Ripken, Jr., Chuck Yeager, and Sam Huff." — *Bob*

Former Cowboys Player/Coach Most Admired and Why

"Roger Staubach - he has continued to be a role model, and gives back to the city of Dallas." — *Bob*

Game Day Rituals

"Get to the stadium early, have the Buck Buchanan Buffet (cold bologna sandwich), and get ready to tape." — *Bob*

My Last Meal Would Be

"Chicken fajitas." — *Bob*

"Macaroni Grill (anything from there)." — *Emily*

Bob & Emily Haas

Assistant Trainer

Philosophy to Live by

"To make the best better." — *Bob*
"Live each day to the fullest." — *Emily*

BORN

Bob - 5-7-69

Emily - 6-3-73

COLLEGE

Bob - West Virginia

YEARS IN NFL

4th Year

Dallas Cowboys

SPOUSE'S OCCUPATION

Case manager for community in schools

Emily and Bob Haas - taken at Fort Worth Botanical Gardens

Best Advice I Could Give to a High School Senior

"Take advantage of a college education. It is something to be very proud of." — *Bob*

"Never let go of your dreams." — *Emily*

What I Value Most

"Friendship." — *Bob*

"My college education." — *Emily*

Best Asset

"Get along with all people." — *Bob*

"I'm easy to talk with." — *Emily*

Favorite Childhood Snack

"Homemade pizza bread." — *Bob*
"Fried cheese." — *Emily*

Favorite Time of Day and Why

"Evening - spending time with my wife." — *Bob*
"Evening - because I am able to spend time with my husband." — *Emily*

Fruit Salad with Honey-Lime Dressing

fresh pineapple, cut into bite-size pieces
cantaloupe, cut into bite-size pieces
watermelon, cut into bite-size pieces
honeydew melon, cut into bite-size pieces
kiwi fruit, peeled and thinly-sliced into rounds
fresh strawberries, washed and hulled
seedless grapes
fresh blueberries

DRESSING

⅓ cup fresh lime juice
⅓ cup honey
1 cup vegetable oil
½ cup dark rum (optional)
½ teaspoon paprika
½ teaspoon powdered mustard
½ teaspoon salt
grated rind of 1 lime

In a large bowl, combine all of the fruit. Cover, and refrigerate. In a small bowl, combine all of the dressing ingredients. Blend well, cover, and refrigerate. Just before serving, pour the dressing over the fruit; toss (to coat). Makes about 2 cups dressing.

Tommy & Cherrie Hart

Assistant Coach
Defensive Ends

Toffee Cake

- ½ cup butter
- ½ cup sugar
- 1 cup brown sugar
- 2 cups sifted flour
- 1 teaspoon baking soda
- ½ teaspoon salt
- 1 cup buttermilk
- 1 egg
- 1 teaspoon vanilla
- 6 Heath bars, frozen and crushed
- ½ cup chopped pecans

Cream butter with sugars. Sift dry ingredients together; add to creamed butter. Put aside ½ cup of this mixture for topping. To the remainder, add buttermilk, egg, and vanilla. Pour batter into greased and floured 13" x 9" pan. To the ½ cup reserved topping, add crushed Heath bars and pecans; spread over the top of batter. Bake at 350 degrees for 30 minutes. Makes 12 servings.

BORN

Tommy - 11-11-44

COLLEGE

Tommy - Morris Brown

CHILDREN

Sebrinna
Ywaketa
Tanya
Crystal

YEARS IN NFL

26 Years
Player:
San Francisco (10)
Chicago (2)
New Orleans (1)
Coach:
San Francisco (11)
Dallas (2)

Biggest Challenge Ever Faced in Life

"Being a parent." — *Steve*

"Leaving my family and great friends in Italy (where I'm from) to come here in the United States to be with the man I adore." — *Raffy*

Three People I Would Invite to a "Fantasy" Dinner Party

"Sam Giancana, Sophia Loren, and Frank Sinatra." — *Steve*

"Barbra Streisand, Mel Gibson, and Antonio Sabato, Jr." — *Raffy*

Favorite City outside of Dallas

"Sirmione, Italy." — *Steve*

"Florence, Italy." — *Raffy*

Mommy and Lucas (one week old)

Hobbies and Other Interests

"Listening to music, watching old movies, reading, and studying Italian." — *Steve*

"Music, reading, and updating and filling our children's scrapbooks with pictures and memories." — *Raffy*

Most Memorable Moment in Life outside of Pro-Football

"Seeing my wife standing in the doorway of the church just before she walked down the aisle." — *Steve*

"The moment when I laid eyes on my babies' faces just seconds after they were born." — *Raffy*

Favorite Time of Day and Why

"Early morning, just as the sun comes up - because of the stillness and serenity in the air." — *Steve*

"Nowadays it's around 10:00 p.m. when, after a busy and fun day with the kids, we put the children to bed, and Steve and I can finally have a few 'seconds' to ourselves (normally spent talking about Mikki and Lucas anyway!)." — *Raffy*

Steve & Raffaella Hoffman

Best Advice I Could Give to a High School Senior

"Think before you act in everything you do, because your life can change in an instant." — *Steve*

"Know yourself, and learn to prioritize - so that among all things in life you won't lose focus on what's important to you and to the people you love." — *Raffy*

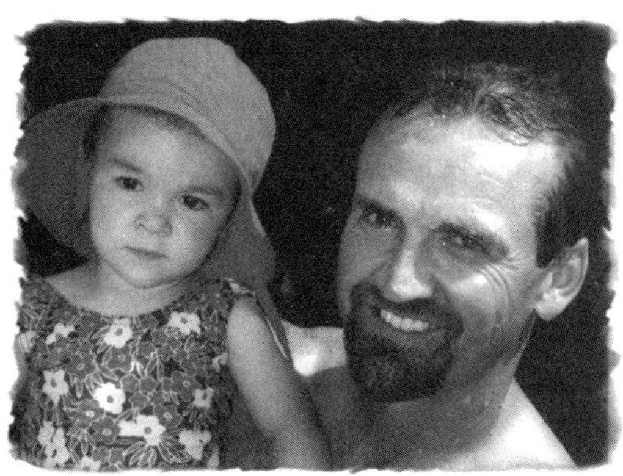

Mikki (20 months old) and Daddy

Philosophy to Live by

"Don't let the good things in life get in the way of the best things in life." — *Steve*

"Help yourself, and God will help you." — *Raffy*

What I Value Most

"Simple, unplanned, and rare moments with friends and family." — *Steve*

"Family, friends, and faith." — *Raffy*

Assistant Coach
Kickers &
Quality Control

BORN

Steve - 9-8-58

Raffaella "Raffy" - 9-23-66

COLLEGE

Steve - Dickinson & St. Thomas

Raffy - Oxford Institute of Languages (Milan, Italy)

ANNIVERSARY

June 13 - 9 years

YEARS IN NFL

9th Year

Dallas Cowboys

SPOUSE'S OCCUPATION

International Flight Attendant - American Airlines

CHILDREN

Micaela - 2 years

Lucas - newborn

PETS

Pongo - 8-year-old Maltese

Cheese Potatoes

6 large potatoes, chopped
½ onion, minced fine
½ poblano pepper or green pepper
2 medium tomatoes, chopped
1 pound box of Velveeta cheese
¼ cup milk
1 jar pimentos
½ teaspoon salt
½ teaspoon pepper
½ teaspoon sugar

Boil together potatoes, onions, and peppers with the salt; drain, when ready. Add pepper, tomatoes, milk, pimentos, sugar; mix it all together with the Velveeta cheese. Serve hot.

Garlic & Rosemary Pork Roast

4 pounds pork roast, boned
4 cloves fresh garlic, pressed
2 teaspoons dried rosemary, crushed *(better if rosemary is fresh)*
3 tablespoons olive oil
1 teaspoon pepper
1 teaspoon salt

Score the top of the roast with deep cuts. Combine all other ingredients; mix well. With basting brush, spread some of the seasoned oil on the roast. Place in 325-degree preheated oven. Bake for 45 minutes to 1 hour per pound (approximately 2½ to 3 hours). Baste several times. Suggestion: To obtain an excellent side dish to accompany this roast, place some chopped potatoes around the roast, sprinkle them with a little bit of rosemary and garlic, and let them cook in the meat juice.

Hudson & Elsie Houck

Assistant
Head Coach
Offensive Line

Philosophy to Live by

"Do what's right, and finish every task." — *Hudson*

Best Advice I Could Give to a High School Senior

"The quality of a person's life is in direct proportion to their commitment to excellence." — *Hudson*

What I Value Most

"Health, happiness, and friendship." — *Hudson*

Best Asset

"Work ethic." — *Hudson*

Biggest Challenge Ever Faced in Life

"Raising children." — *Hudson*

If I Were Not in Professional Football I Would Be

"In a team-oriented business." — *Hudson*

Three People I Would Invite to a "Fantasy" Dinner Party

"Al Pacino, Arnold Palmer, and Michael Jordan." — *Hudson*

Former Cowboys Player/Coach Most Admired and Why

"Tom Landry - commitment to the game." — *Hudson*

Favorite Pre-Game or Post-Game Meal

Post-Game - "Mexican food." — *Hudson*

BORN

Hudson - 1-7-43

Elsie - 12-22-47

COLLEGE

Hudson - USC

Elsie - Virginia

YEARS IN NFL

15th Year

Dallas Cowboys (5)

Los Angeles Rams (9)

Seattle Seahawks (1)

SPOUSE'S OCCUPATION

Banker

ANNIVERSARY

June 15 - 6 years

CHILDREN

Troy - 31 years

Scott - 28 years

Holly - 25 years

At Newport Beach, California, while on vacation - left to right:
Ali (friend); Scott; Holly; Lucille (Hudson's mom); Elsie; and Hudson

My Last Meal Would Be

"Grilled salmon and crab legs." — *Hudson*

"Crab legs." — *Elsie*

Favorite Childhood Snack

"Ice cream." — *Hudson*

"Cookies." — *Elsie*

Favorite City outside of Dallas

"San Diego, California." — *Hudson*

Hobbies and Other Interests

"Golf, travel, and reading." — *Hudson*

"Golf, skiing, scuba diving, travel, and movies." — *Elsie*

Most Memorable Moment in Life outside of Pro-Football

"Playing football on a National Championship team." — *Hudson*

Favorite Time of Day and Why

"Morning - energy level is high." — *Hudson*

Capitol Chicken

4 tablespoons butter
1 tablespoon oil
8 chicken breasts, split
1 tablespoon flour
1 can (10½-ounce) cream of chicken soup
1 cup white wine
1 cup water
½ cup whipping cream
1 teaspoon salt
¼ teaspoon tarragon leave
¼ teaspoon pepper
1 can (15-ounce) artichoke hearts
6 green onions
2 tablespoons parsley, chopped

Place butter and oil in skillet; heat, over medium heat. Add chicken; sauté, until browned on both sides. Transfer chicken to baking pan or casserole. In same skillet, sauté fresh mushrooms (sliced) for 5 minutes. Stir in flour; add soup, wine, and water. Stir, while simmering, until sauce thickens. Stir in cream, salt, tarragon, and pepper; pour over chicken. Bake, uncovered at 350 degrees for 1 hour. Mix; add artichoke hearts, green onions, and parsley. Bake an additional 5 minutes, or until chicken is fork-tender. Makes 8 servings.

Artichoke Dip

1 can, or frozen package, artichoke hearts
1 cup mayonnaise
½ cup Parmesan cheese
garlic powder, to taste
paprika

Mix all ingredients together. Bake at 325 degrees for 20 minutes. Sprinkle paprika on top.

Biggest Challenge Ever Faced in Life

"Quitting drinking." —*Joe*

"Being a parent." — *Camille*

If I Were Not in Professional Football I Would Be

"Coaching at a different level." —*Joe*

Three People I Would Invite to a "Fantasy" Dinner Party

"Dennis Rodman, Willem DaFoe, and Christopher Walken." —*Joe*

Former Cowboys Player/Coach Most Admired and Why

"Roger Staubach - his ability to succeed." —*Joe*

"Greg Johnson - because he's a good friend, and he is incredibly funny." — *Camille*

Game Day Rituals

"Up early (4:30 a.m.), have breakfast, and stretch - stretch - stretch, and game face." —*Joe*

"Everything that a mother with young children would do." — *Camille*

My Last Meal Would Be

"Cappellini with red sauce." —*Joe*

"Patsy's (my dad) lobster." — *Camille*

Favorite Childhood Snack

"Hostess cupcake and milk." —*Joe*

"A Devil Dog." — *Camille*

Favorite Holiday or Holiday Tradition

"Fourth of July - barbecue." —*Joe*

"Christmas Eve - a traditional Italian dinner with my dysfunctional family (ha-ha!)." — *Camille*

Most Memorable Moment in Life outside of Pro-Football

"The day my kids were born." —*Joe*

"Creating a famous haircut." — *Camille*

Joseph D. "Joe" & Camille Juruszek

Assistant Coach Strength & Conditioning

Philosophy to Live by

"Just don't worry about it." — *Joe*

"In life, always go forward, not backward, and what goes around, comes around." — *Camille*

Camille and Joe Juruszek

BORN

Joe - 6-8-58

Camille - 9-20-60

COLLEGE

Joe - New Mexico & Oklahoma

Camille - Duncan Bros. Hair Design

YEARS IN NFL

1st Year

Dallas Cowboys

SPOUSE'S OCCUPATION

Hair Stylist, salon owner, & CEO of household

ANNIVERSARY

March 12 - 10 years

CHILDREN

Nikki Jo - 7 years

J.D. - 5 years

Best Advice I Could Give to a High School Senior

"Don't ever leave school, and don't grow up." — *Joe*

"Fulfill your life dreams before marriage and children, so you don't ever feel like you've missed out." — *Camille*

What I Value Most

"My family." — *Joe*

"My marriage, and my kids." — *Camille*

Best Asset

"My big ears." — *Joe*

"High morals and values." — *Camille*

Pasta and Broccoli

1 head of broccoli
1 package penne pasta
1 large can Progresso whole tomatoes
½ cup olive oil (extra virgin - First Cold Press)
6 large garlic cloves
1 tablespoon basil
1 teaspoon salt
pinch, or more, red pepper
Parmesan cheese

In a pot, put olive oil with sliced garlic pieces (not chopped or minced); brown well. Once the garlic is browned, add your smashed tomatoes, salt, pepper, and basil; cook for 30 minutes. In a separate pot, steam broccoli; cook, until you can break with a fork (do not overcook). Boil pasta in salted water (1 tablespoon salt), until aldente. When pasta is ready, drain. Add broccoli and sauce in the pot; toss. Serve with Parmesan cheese.

Twice-Baked Potatoes

2 large potatoes
½ bunch scallion onions
2 tablespoons sour cream
½ package shredded Monterey Jack cheese
½ stick butter
salt, to taste
Lawry's seasoned pepper, to taste

Bake potatoes for 1 hour at 400 degrees. Slice opening on top of potato; remove inside of potato, leaving the shell. In a bowl, mix all of the ingredients together; stuff potato. Put back in oven; bake at 350 degrees for 15 minutes. Serve.

Jim D. & Rosanne Maurer

Head Athletic Trainer

Best Advice I Could Give to a High School Senior

"Your learning years are not ending - they are just beginning." — *Jim*

"Be true to yourself - study what you love - stay open!!! - and always be a student of life." — *Rosanne*

Ben, Nick, and Jim - the boys ganging up on daddy after work

Philosophy to Live by

"You will never have enough time for everything. If you want time, you must make it." —*Jim*

"The life that is not examined is not worth living (Plato)." — *Rosanne*

What I Value Most

"Time spent with my family." —*Jim*

"Relationship with God, and family." — *Rosanne*

BORN

Jim - 3-8-65

Rosanne - 2-23-65

COLLEGE

Jim - SMU

Rosanne - Texas Tech

YEARS IN NFL

9th Year

Dallas Cowboys

SPOUSE'S OCCUPATION

Homemaker

ANNIVERSARY

December 7 - 6 years

CHILDREN

Nick - 8 years

Ben - 5 years

PETS

Rookie - Silky Terrier

Rosanne, Ben, and Nick (holding Rookie) -
at home, celebrating Ben's 5th birthday with family

Biggest Challenge Ever Faced in Life

"Responsibility of parenthood." —*Jim*

"Living life one day at a time. Today is a gift from God - that's why we call it the present." — *Rosanne*

Three People We Would Invite to a "Fantasy" Dinner Party

"Lucille Ball, Steve McQueen, and the cheerleading duo from Saturday Night Live!" —*Jim and Rosanne*

Game Day Rituals

"Right ankle first, if possible." —*Jim*

My Last Meal Would Be

"Tony Roma's ribs (baby back) and baked potato." —*Jim*

"Mostaccioli, Italian green beans, and garlic bread." — *Rosanne*

Favorite Childhood Snack

"Homemade vanilla ice cream, Hershey's chocolate syrup, and pecan pieces." —*Jim*

"Red licorice - after swimming at the Knights of Columbus." — *Rosanne*

Most Memorable Moment in Life outside of Pro-Football

"In the delivery room - seeing my two sons for the first time." — *Rosanne*

Marinated Pasta Salad

8 ounces tri-color rotini spirals pasta
½ pound, fresh or frozen, asparagus (cooked 5 to 7 minutes, and cut into 1-inch pieces)
½ cup cut-up red pepper
½ cup cut-up zucchini
½ cup finely-chopped red onion
½ cup thinly-sliced celery
¼ teaspoon salt
⅛ teaspoon ground black pepper
¼ cup Italian dressing

Cook pasta, according to package directions; rinse, drain, and cool. Place in a large bowl; add vegetables, and toss to mix. Add remaining ingredients. Toss, cover, and refrigerate for several hours, or overnight. Serve on leaf lettuce. Makes 8 servings.

Low-Fat Quesadillas

12 fat-free tortillas (flour or corn)
1 can fat-free refried beans
1 onion, thinly-sliced
pickled jalapeno slices
fat-free Cheddar cheese, shredded

Spread a thick layer of beans on a tortilla. Place onion and jalapeno slices on top of beans. Sprinkle cheese over all; top with another tortilla. Heat a non-stick skillet, on medium; place quesadilla (cheese side down), and cook, until crispy. Flip; cook, until the second side is crispy. Repeat - until all tortillas are cooked. Serve hot with salsa.

Biggest Challenge Ever Faced in Life

"Maintaining a positive attitude during difficult life experiences." — *Bruce*

"Going back to graduate school after eleven years of raising a family." — *Kathy*

Mays' daughter - Laura (19 years)

Three People I Would Invite to a "Fantasy" Dinner Party

"Patton, Powell, and Swartzkoff." — *Bruce*

Former Cowboys Player/Coach Most Admired and Why

"Neill Armstrong - a good person with integrity." — *Bruce*

Favorite Holiday or Holiday Tradition

"Christmas." — *Bruce*

"Watching white Christmas with my family." — *Kathy*

Mays' daughter - Jennifer (22 years)

Hobbies and Other Interests

"Golf, reading about successful people, and listening to educational tapes." — *Bruce*

Most Memorable Moment in Life outside of Pro-Football

"The day Kathy and I got married." — *Bruce*

Favorite Time of Day and Why

"Early morning - when I'm most alert." — *Bruce*

"Evening - when I can spend time with my husband." — *Kathy*

Bruce B. & Kathryn "Kathy" Mays

Dallas Cowboys
Front Office Staff
Director of
Operations

Best Advice I Could Give to a High School Senior

"Be knowledgeable, open to ideas, and continue to learn." — *Bruce*

"Work hard today, so you can have choices tomorrow." — *Kathy*

Bruce and Kathy Mays - enjoying themselves at the Christmas party at Gene and Jerry Jones' home

Philosophy to Live by

"Be true to your principles." — *Bruce*

"Never quit." — *Kathy*

What I Value Most

"Trust." — *Bruce*

"Honesty." — *Kathy*

Best Asset

"Trustworthiness." — *Bruce*

"Dependable." — *Kathy*

BORN

Bruce - 8-6-43

Kathy - 1-6-48

COLLEGE

Bruce -
Ohio Northern - Akron; &
Oklahoma State (Ph.D.)

Kathy - Oklahoma State

YEARS IN NFL

8th Year

Dallas Cowboys

SPOUSE'S OCCUPATION

Registered dietitian

ANNIVERSARY

May 7 - 15 years

CHILDREN

Kirsten - 28 years

Jennifer - 22 years

Laura - 19 years

Damien - 19 years

PETS

Shakespeare - Toy Poodle

Bruce's Shrimp 'n Rice

1 onion, chopped
2 ribs of celery, chopped
1 small green pepper, chopped
1 cup cooked rice
1 cup grated sharp cheese
1 can (10¼ ounce) cream of mushroom soup
½ pound cooked shrimp
lemon
paprika
olive oil

Sauté onion, celery, and green pepper in small amount of olive oil. Mix with rice, cheese, soup, and shrimp. Put ingredients in a casserole dish; top with thinly-sliced lemon. Sprinkle with paprika. Bake at 350 degrees, until casserole bubbles. Makes 4 servings.

Kathy's Philly Fruit Pizza

1 tube Pillsbury Sugar Cookie dough (let stand 15 minutes before using)
1 package (8-ounce) cream cheese, softened
⅓ cup sugar
½ teaspoon vanilla
assorted fruits

Pat dough into pizza pan; bake 8 to 10 minutes. Let cool completely. Spread mixture of sugar, cream cheese, and vanilla onto crust. Arrange assorted fruits on top of pizza in a design of choice.

Mike & Jan McCord

Equipment Manager

Philosophy to Live by

"Live every moment to its fullest." — *Mike*
"Do unto others as you would want them to do unto you." — *Jan*

Jan and Mike - with two family dogs, Jasper and Sheba

BORN

Mike - 11-6-64

Jan - 2-20-63

COLLEGE

Mike - Texas

Jan - West Texas State

YEARS IN NFL

9th Year

Dallas Cowboys

SPOUSE'S OCCUPATION

Bookkeeper for home builder

ANNIVERSARY

May 21 - 3 years

PETS

Sheba - Sheltie

Jasper - Chihuahua

Best Advice I Could Give to a High School Senior

"Take your education very seriously." — *Mike*

"Make the most of your senior year and your education." — *Jan*

What I Value Most

"My and my wife's health." — *Mike*

"Family." — *Jan*

Best Asset

"My easy-going personality." — *Mike*

Chocolate Cake

2 cups flour
2 cups sugar
1¼ teaspoons baking soda
½ cup cocoa
1 cup Wesson oil
2 eggs
1 cup buttermilk
1 cup hot water
¼ teaspoon salt
2 teaspoons vanilla

Into a large bowl, sift all of the dry ingredients; pour in oil and beat. Add beaten eggs, buttermilk, and vanilla. Lastly, add hot water; beat well. Bake at 350 degrees, just until cake springs back in center (approximately 20 to 25 minutes). Makes 36 cup cakes or large layer cake.

*Makes great cup cakes!

Biggest Challenge Ever Faced in Life

"The death of my grandfather, John Chandler." — *Mike*

"Moving away from home and my friends and family to come to Dallas for my job." —*Jan*

If I Were Not in Professional Football I Would Be

"An athletic director for a small college in a small town." — *Mike*

Three People I Would Invite to a "Fantasy" Dinner Party

"Michael Jordan, Tom Cruise, and Sandra Bullock." — *Mike*

Former Cowboys Player/Coach Most Admired and Why

"Randy White - for personality and his work ethic." — *Mike*

Game Day Rituals

"Never shave on game day; 2-way taping the shoulder pads for Tuinei, Bates, Tolbert, and other veteran players (in numerical order); and putting Emmitt Smith's jersey on his shoulder pads." — *Mike*

My Last Meal Would Be

"Chicken-fried steak and mashed potatoes." — *Mike*

"Steak and baked potato." —*Jan*

Favorite Childhood Snack

"Chocolate chip cookies." — *Mike*

"Potato chips." —*Jan*

Favorite Holiday or Holiday Tradition

"Fourth of July - because I don't have to work this holiday - unlike Christmas or Thanksgiving." — *Mike*

"Christmas." —*Jan*

Favorite City outside of Dallas

"Lake Tahoe, Nevada." — *Mike*

Hobbies and Other Interests

"Golf, movies, country music and dancing, and yard work around the house." — *Mike*

"Dancing, movies, country music, water sports, and antique shopping." —*Jan*

Most Memorable Moment in Life outside of Pro-Football

"My wedding day, and graduation from college." — *Mike*

"Wedding day." —*Jan*

Favorite Time of Day and Why

"9:00 p.m. - it is quiet time at home with my wife and dogs before going to bed." — *Mike*

"Evening - most relaxing time of the day and time to reflect on the day." —*Jan*

Scalloped Potatoes

- 2 tablespoons butter
- 1 tablespoon all-purpose flour
- 1½ cups milk
- 1 teaspoon salt
- ¼ teaspoon pepper
- 4 cups thinly-sliced, peeled potatoes (about 2 pounds)
- 1 medium onion, finely-chopped
- 1 small green pepper, finely-chopped
- buttered bread crumbs
- shredded Cheddar cheese

In a saucepan, melt butter; stir in flour. Add milk (all at once), stirring constantly. Cook and stir, over low heat, until thickened and bubbly. In a greased 1½-quart baking dish, arrange half the potatoes, onion, and green pepper in layers; cover with half of the sauce. Repeat layers. Cover and bake at 350 degrees for 35 minutes. Sprinkle with buttered bread crumbs. Bake, uncovered, about 40 minutes longer, or until potatoes are tender. Sprinkle with Cheddar cheese. Let stand for 5 minutes before serving. Makes 4 to 6 servings.

Favorite Childhood Snack

"Chocolate milk shake." — *Clancy*

Favorite Holiday or Holiday Tradition

"Christmas." — *Clancy*

Favorite City outside of Dallas

"La Jolla, California." — *Clancy*

Hobbies and Other Interests

"Jogging, watching TV and movies, and traveling." — *Clancy*

Clancy Pendergast

Defensive Assistant
Quality Control

Philosophy to Live by

"Always use good judgment." — *Clancy*

Clancy Pendergast and his dad - at the Kentucky Derby (1997)

BORN

11-29-67

COLLEGE

Arizona

YEARS IN NFL

3rd Year

Dallas Cowboys (2)

Houston Oilers (1)

Best Advice I Could Give to a High School Senior

"Get a college education." — *Clancy*

What I Value Most

"My family." — *Clancy*

Best Asset

"Having great parents." — *Clancy*

If I Were Not in Professional Football I Would Be

"Running a dairy farm." — *Clancy*

My Last Meal Would Be

"Mexican food." — *Clancy*

German Apple Cake

3 cups all-purpose flour
3 teaspoons baking powder
1 teaspoon salt
4 eggs
2 cups sugar
1 cup vegetable oil
½ cup orange juice
2½ teaspoons vanilla
4 cups thinly-sliced, peeled apples (about 4 to 5 apples)
2 teaspoons ground cinnamon
3 tablespoons sugar
powdered sugar, optional

Combine the first three ingredients; set aside. In a large mixing bowl, beat eggs and sugar. Combine oil and orange juice; add (alternating with dry ingredients) to egg/sugar mixture. Mix, until smooth; add vanilla, and beat well. Pour half of the batter into a greased and floured tube pan. Arrange half the apples over the batter. Combine cinnamon and sugar; sprinkle half over the apples. Top with remaining batter, apples, and cinnamon/sugar. Bake at 350 degrees for 1 hour and 10 minutes, or until cake tests done. Allow cake to cool for 1 hour before removing from baking pan. Cool, apple side up, on a wire rack. Sprinkle top with powdered sugar, if desired. Makes 12 to 16 servings.

Bill & D'Ann Priakos

Director of Merchandising

Philosophy to Live by

"Work hard, and play hard." — *Bill*
"Always be fair and honest." — *D'Ann*

Bill and D'Ann Priakos

Best Advice I Could Give to a High School Senior

"Work hard, and good things will happen." — *Bill*

"Don't be afraid to chase your dreams." — *D'Ann*

What I Value Most

"My family." — *Bill and D'Ann*

Best Asset

"My wife." — *Bill*

"My husband." — *D'Ann*

BORN

Bill - 1-19-65

D'Ann - 12-3-67

COLLEGE

Bill - Arkansas

D'Ann - LSU

YEARS IN NFL

1st Year

Dallas Cowboys

SPOUSE'S OCCUPATION

Director of Merchandisers - Ruff Hewn Company

ANNIVERSARY

January 30 - 4 years

CHILDREN

Expecting first child on October 7, 1997

PETS

Misha - Siberian Husky

Kitty - Cat

Biggest Challenge Ever Faced in Life

"Preparing for the birth of my son." — *Bill*

"Pregnancy." — *D'Ann*

Three People I Would Invite to a "Fantasy" Dinner Party

"Dan Patrick (ESPN), Tiger Woods, and John McEnroe." — *Bill*

Former Cowboys Player/Coach Most Admired and Why

"Roger Staubach - leader on and off the field." — *Bill*

"Roger Staubach - he was a winner." — *D'Ann*

My Last Meal Would Be

"A huge medium-rare filet." — *Bill*

"Boiled crawfish." — *D'Ann*

Favorite Childhood Snack

"Chocolate chip cookies." — *Bill*

"Candy." — *D'Ann*

Favorite Holiday or Holiday Tradition

"Christmas." — *Bill and D'Ann*

Favorite City outside of Dallas

"Cozumel, Mexico." — *Bill*

"New Orleans, Louisiana." — *D'Ann*

Bill and D'Ann - at Jackson Hole, Wyoming (March 1, 1996)

Hobbies and Other Interests

"Scuba diving, snow skiing, and golf." — *Bill*

"Scuba diving, snow skiing, and relaxing with family and friends." — *D'Ann*

Most Memorable Moment in Life outside of Pro-Football

"When I learned my wife was pregnant with our first child." — *Bill*

"My wedding." — *D'Ann*

Favorite Time of Day and Why

"Evening - relaxing with my wife." — *Bill*

"Evening - relaxing and unwinding at home with my husband." — *D'Ann*

Crawfish Etouffee

¼ pound butter
2 large onions, chopped
2 stalks celery, chopped
2 cloves garlic, minced
salt and pepper, to taste
Tabasco sauce, to taste
1 medium bell pepper, chopped
1 pound crawfish tails
4 tablespoons flour
2 cups water
4 chicken bouillon cubes
1 bunch green onions, chopped

Melt butter in a large skillet; sauté vegetables in butter for 30 minutes. Add salt, pepper, and Tabasco, to taste. Add crawfish tails; sauté for 1 minute. Stir in flour; continue to sauté for 3 minutes. Add water, chicken bouillon cubes, and green onions; simmer for 10 to 15 minutes. Serve over rice. Makes 4 to 6 servings. "Bon Appetit."

Three People I Would Invite to a "Fantasy" Dinner Party

"John Muir, Benjamin Franklin, and Nelson Mandela." —*Jack*

Former Cowboys Player/Coach Most Admired and Why

"Roger Staubach - persistence, spirit, and productivity." —*Jack*

My Last Meal Would Be

"Salmon dinner with baked potato, Beringer Chardonnay, and carrot cake with ice cream." —*Jack*

"Hot fudge sundae." — *Wendy*

Favorite Childhood Snack

"Apple slices - just kidding! - Oreo cookies." —*Jack*

"Frozen banana on Balboa Island, California." — *Wendy*

Jack and Wendy Reilly and family

Favorite City outside of Dallas

"Ketchum, Idaho." —*Jack*

"Kapalua, Hawaii." — *Wendy*

Hobbies and Other Interests

"Fly fishing, golfing, reading, and traveling." —*Jack*

"Hiking, and reading." — *Wendy*

Jack & Wendy Reilly

Assistant Coach
Quarterbacks

Philosophy to Live by

"Work hard - play hard." — *Jack*

Jack Reilly - in float tube

BORN

Jack - 5-22-45

COLLEGE

Jack - Cal State - Long Beach & Azusa Pacific

Wendy - Cal State - Long Beach

YEARS IN NFL

8th Year

Dallas Cowboys (1)

San Diego Chargers (4)

Los Angeles Raiders (1)

St. Louis Rams (2)

SPOUSE'S OCCUPATION

Teacher

ANNIVERSARY

July 29 - 30 years

CHILDREN

Chris - 26 years

Corrie - 25 years

Katie - 20 years

Best Advice I Could Give to a High School Senior

"Finish college, and pursue interests that you love." —*Jack*

What I Value Most

"Family." —*Jack*

Best Asset

"Patience." —*Jack*

Biggest Challenge Ever Faced in Life

"Trying to beat Troy and Ernie in a golf match - with Hudson as my partner." —*Jack*

If I Were Not in Professional Football I Would Be

"Fly-fishing guide - Silver Creek, Idaho." —*Jack*

Lewis and Clark's White Chili

- 3 pounds cooked Great Northern beans, canned or bottled
- 2 pounds boneless chicken breasts, skin removed
- 1 tablespoon olive oil
- 4 garlic cloves, minced
- 2 medium onions, chopped
- 2 teaspoons ground cumin
- ¼ teaspoon ground cloves
- ¼ teaspoon cayenne pepper
- 1 teaspoon ground oregano
- 2 cans (4-ounce) chopped mild green chilies
- 20 ounces Monterey Jack cheese, grated
- sour cream
- chopped jalapeno peppers, canned

In large saucepan, place chicken; add cold water to cover, and bring to a simmer. Cook, until tender (approximately 15 to 20 minutes). Remove from saucepan; dice into ½-inch cubes. Using the same pan, discard water; and heat oil, over medium heat. Add onions, until translucent. Stir in garlic, chilies, cumin, cayenne pepper, oregano, and cloves; sauté for 2 to 3 minutes. Add chicken, beans, stock, and 12 ounces of cheese; let simmer for 15 minutes. Ladle into large bowls; top with 1 ounce of cheese. Serve with a side of sour cream and chopped jalapeno peppers. Makes 6 to 8 servings.

Easy Dessert Fondue

Cut chunks of fruit - strawberries, bananas, pineapple, etc. Dip in sour cream; then, in brown sugar or shaved chocolate.

Ernie & Joyce Zampese

Assistant Coach
Offensive
Coordinator

Best Advice I Could Give to a High School Senior

"Set goals and attack them with passion." — *Ernie*

"Try all your dreams." — *Joyce*

Ernie and Joyce Zampese - at Cowboys' football party (Christmas 1996)

Philosophy to Live by

"Treat others with respect." — *Ernie*

What I Value Most

"Family." — *Ernie*

"Faith, family, and friends." — *Joyce*

Best Asset

"Even temperament." — *Ernie*

Biggest Challenge Ever Faced in Life

"Marriage and children." — *Joyce*

BORN

Ernie - 3-12-35

Joyce - 11-23

COLLEGE

Ernie - USC, Cal Poly - San Luis Obispo

Joyce - Marymount College - Westwood, UC - Santa Barbara & Cal Poly - San Luis Obispo

YEARS IN NFL

19th Year

Dallas Cowboys (4)

Los Angeles Rams (7)

San Diego Chargers (8)

SPOUSE'S OCCUPATION

Homemaker

ANNIVERSARY

July 2 - 37 years

CHILDREN

Kristen - 35 years

Laurie - 33 years

Ken - 30 years

Jon - 22 years

Former Cowboys Player/Coach Most Admired and Why

"Roger Staubach and Tom Landry - won with class." —*Ernie*

Game Day Rituals

"Mass, go to game with Elsie, watch the game, and go to dinner with friends." —*Joyce*

My Last Meal Would Be

"Steak and lobster." —*Ernie*

"Macaroni and cheese." —*Joyce*

Three beautiful ladies: Kristen (daughter), Christine (daughter-in-law), and Laurie (daughter)

Favorite Childhood Snack

"Italian candy." —*Ernie*

"Bubble gum." —*Joyce*

Hobbies and Other Interests

"Reading, family gatherings, and barbecuing." —*Ernie*

"Reading, sewing, and family get-togethers." —*Joyce*

Most Memorable Moment in Life outside of Pro-Football

"Birth of first child." —*Ernie*

Favorite Time of Day and Why

"Early morning." —*Ernie and Joyce*

Judy Epplers' Hawaiian Torte

vanilla wafers
1 cube margarine, softened
1 box (1-pound) powdered sugar
2 eggs
medium-size can crushed pineapple
2 packages Dream Whip
¾ cup walnuts, chopped

Crush vanilla wafers; put one-half wafers on bottom of buttered 13" x 9" glass dish. Take margarine, powdered sugar, and eggs; beat until creamy. Spread on bottom layer crust. Drain crushed pineapple; spread over mixture. Whip Dream Whip, until it peaks; spread over mixture. Sprinkle chopped walnuts over the top; spread rest of crushed wafers over the top. Chill until firm. Can be frozen.

Newest grandchild: Marina Kathleen Zampese - daughter of Ken and Christine (born 11-16-96)

Best Asset

"Work ethic, and tenacity." — *Mike*

"Loving and caring for my family." — *Vikki*

Biggest Challenge Ever Faced in Life

"Learning to play golf." — *Mike*

"Being the best mom and wife that I can be." — *Vikki*

Three People I Would Invite to a "Fantasy" Dinner Party

"Mike's 99-year-old grandfather (*we lost this year*), Vince Lombardi, and Michael Jordan." — *Mike*

Former Cowboys Player/Coach Most Admired and Why

"Tom Landry - because of his class, leadership, and family values." — *Vikki*

Game Day Rituals

"Go to stadium early, sit and be nervous in the locker room, never eat, and play game in my mind before the game." — *Mike*

"Go to church and pray, tailgate with Marki and Corri, and cheer Cowboys on to victory." — *Vikki*

My Last Meal Would Be

"Crab legs." — *Mike*

"Shrimp Scampi and red wine." — *Vikki*

Favorite Childhood Snack

"Chocolate chip cookies." — *Mike*

"Graham crackers with icing." — *Vikki*

Favorite City outside of Dallas

"Super Bowl city." — *Mike*

"Ogden Canyon, Utah - because of mountains." — *Vikki*

Favorite Time of Day and Why

"Early in the morning - because no one bothers me." — *Mike*

"After dropping the kids off at school - having my coffee, because it gives me a half-hour to myself." — *Vikki*

Mike & Vikki Zimmer

Philosophy to Live by

"Work hard, always give best effort, and be a good person." — *Mike*

"Respect, manners, and say a prayer for the next day." — *Vikki*

The Zimmer family - celebrating a win over the Patriots - at San Francisco Steak House (1996)

Best Advice I Could Give to a High School Senior

"Enjoy yourself, and work to be the best you can." — *Mike*

"Work hard, stay out of trouble, and ask for help from above." — *Vikki*

What I Value Most

"My family." — *Mike*

"My husband, my children, and Mike's and my families." — *Vikki*

Assistant Coach
Defensive Backs

BORN

Mike - 6-5-56

Vikki - 6-9-59

COLLEGE

Mike - Illinois State

Vikki - Weber State & Utah

SPOUSE'S OCCUPATION

Housewife and mom

CHILDREN

Adam William - 13 years

Marki Nichole - 10 years

Corri Dawn - 7 years

PETS

Hunter - Yellow Lab

T.D. - Toy Poodle

YEARS IN NFL

4th Year

Dallas Cowboys

Vikki's One-Pan Potatoes and Chicken Dijon

4 medium-size potatoes, sliced ¼-inch thick (microwave, for 8 to 10 minutes, until tender)
1 pound chicken breasts (boneless and skinless), sliced 1-inch thick
2 tablespoons vegetable oil
¼ cup prepared honey-Dijon barbecue sauce
1 teaspoon dried tarragon

In a large skillet (while potatoes cook), toss and brown chicken in oil, over high heat, for 5 minutes. Add potatoes; sauté and toss, until potatoes are lightly-browned. Add barbecue sauce and tarragon; toss, until heated through (about 20 minutes). Makes 4 servings.

Zimmer Kids' Jell-O Popcorn

1 cup sugar
1 cup Karo syrup
1 small package of any flavor Jell-O
popcorn, popped

In saucepan, combine all of the ingredients; boil for 3 minutes. Pour over 3 to 4 quarts of popped popcorn.
* Great after-school snack!

Recipe Index

Appetizers & Dips

Artichoke Dip, 271
Conna's Corn Dip, 190
Crab Meat Dip, 98
Jeff Brodsky's Hot (No-Fry) Crispy Wings, 244
Low-Fat Quesadillas, 277
Olive Oil and Balsamic Bread Dip, 232
Shrimp Dip, 161
Shrimp Spring Rolls, 105
Star Cheese Bites, 173
Unique Deviled Eggs, 132

Bread & Muffins

Almond Danish, 52
Banana Bread, 141
Chocolate Banana Bread, 128
Double-Chocolate Waffles, 106
Gingerbread, 30
Jalapeno Cornbread Muffins, 182
Jason and Brill's Baked French Toast, 86
Orange Muffins, 180

Desserts

Amaretto Cheesecake, 165
Apple Cherry Cobbler, 179
Apple Cider Pound Cake, 133
Awesome Brownies, 206
Chocolate-Blueberry Squares, 176
Chocolate Cake, 282
Chocolate Layered Dessert, 220
Chocolate No-Bake Cookies, 128
Choice Apple Cake, 100
Coconut Pie, 216
Cream Cheese Tarts, 80
Devil's Food Cake, 89
Easy Dessert Fondue, 292
Eggnog Pie, 44
German Apple Cake, 286
Honey Crunch Cookies, 71
Incomparable Bread Pudding, 124
Judy Epplers' Hawaiian Torte, 295
Kathy's Philly Fruit Pizza, 280
Lemon Poppy Seed Cake, 224
Lemon Pound Cake - with a Twist, 13
Miracle Bars, 196
Old-Fashioned Peach Cobbler, 146
Pear and Hazelnut Tarts, 5
Pineapple Cake, 250
Pumpkin Pie in Spiced Nut Crust, 203
Rhubarb Pie, 149
Special Cookies, 63
Toffee Cake, 265
Troy's Favorite Chocolate Chip Cookies, 26

Main Dishes & Casseroles

Baby Back Ribs, 255
Baked Stuffed Flounder, 93
Barbecued Pork Chops, 210
Barbecued Spareribs, 145
Beef Supper, 25
Bow-Tie Pasta, 47
Breakfast Burritos, 39
Britt's Mom's Chicken Spaghetti, 249
Bruce's Shrimp 'n Rice, 280
Buttermilk Baked Chicken, 229

Capitol Chicken, 271
Chicken and Asparagus Casserole, 174
Chicken and Dumplings, 39
Chicken and Dumplings in Herbed Broth, 138
Chicken Marinade, 256
Chicken Marsala, 157
Chicken Pot Pie, 219
Chicken Teriyaki, 262
Chicken with Cucumbers in Paprika Sauce, 64
Chili, 75
Crab Cakes Maryland, 238
Crawfish Etouffe, 289
Crawfish Fettucine, 216
Crawfish Fettucini, 122
Flounder Grilled in Foil, 190
Garlic and Rosemary Pork Roast, 268
Ham and Potatoes au Gratin, 129
Herb-Baked Catfish, 114
Honey-Lemon Chicken, 110
Impossible Taco Pie, 196
Italian Eggs, 18
Lasagna, 12
Limeade Grilled Chicken, 60
Marinated/Grilled Lamb Chops, 99
Mexican Lasagna, 243
Mexican-Style Pork Ribs, 130
Our Friend Fran's Flank Steak Marinade, 261
Pasta and Sausage Dish, 249
Quiche, 80
Rotel Chicken, 43
Salmon Croquettes, 152
Santa Fe Chicken, 250
Savory Crab Cakes, 170
Shrimp Etouffee, 169
Singor's Dishwasher Salmon, 141
Southwestern Omelet, 16
Spicy Catfish, 224
Spring Primavera, 60
Tamale Pie, 29
Vikki's One-Pan Potatoes and Chicken Dijon, 298
Zesty Meatloaf, 237

Salads

All-American Creamy Coleslaw, 137
Black-Eyed Peas and Shrimp Salad, 113
Caesar Salad, 158
Chicken Fajita Salad, 153
Chicken Salad, 40
Fruit Salad with Honey-Lime Dressing, 264
Marinated Pasta Salad, 277

Sandwiches

Crab Bake Sandwich, 212
Fantastic Burgers, 97
French Dip Sandwiches, 206
Special Hamburgers, 33

Sauces

Joe's Florida Stone Crab Mustard Sauce, 238

Side Dishes

Baked Beans Western-Style, 209
Beefy Baked Beans, 33
Cauliflower Bake, 55
Cheese Potatoes, 268

Corn Pudding, 261
Cornbread Sausage Stuffing with Apples, 118
Fresh Corn Pudding, 185
Grits Supreme Casserole, 98
Orange Carrots, 82
Oven-Roasted Potatoes, 82
Pasta and Broccoli, 274
Pasta Fagioli, 19
Rice and Artichoke Casserole, 9
Rustic Potato Wedges, 256
Scalloped Potatoes, 284
Spanish Rice, 51
Spinach Casserole, 161
Superior Squash Casserole, 93
Twice-Baked Potatoes, 274
Vegetable-Rice Casserole, 26

Snacks & Beverages

French Chocolate, 212
Lemonade, 75
Pralines, 122
Zimmer Kids' Jell-O Popcorn, 298

Soups

Cascadilla Soup, 5
Gazpacho, 234
Lewis & Clark's White Chili, 292
Minestrone Soup, 200
Mr. C's Seafood Gumbo, 68
Old-Fashioned Potato Soup, 29
Potato/Cheddar Cheese Soup, 70
Wisconsin Cheese Soup, 110

Our Grateful Appreciation to our Sponsors

from the Students at Happy Hill Farm Academy/Home

Access Creative/Web Life Productions 204
Troy Aikman Foundation 56
Bob & Mary Breunig 48
Bryan 150
The Official Dallas Cowboys Pro Shop 186
Dallas Cowboys Travel 134
The Dallas Cowboys Weekly 142
The Dallas Cowboys Wives Association 72
Danka 90
Delta Airlines 34
Desktop Miracles, Inc. 226
Interstate Batteries 162
David McDavid Auto Group 166
Mobil 22
National Door Industries, Inc. 154
James D. Smith Photography 72
Starwood 2
Tom Thumb 20
Trophy Inspirational Publishers Outlet 94
Walls Industries, Inc. 76

listed alphabetically

ORDER EXTRA COPIES NOW!

Cowboys' fans, friends, memorabilia collectors, and
good cooks that you know will love a copy of this limited-edition

Dallas Cowboys Wives
The Dallas Cowboys Family "Playbook"

To Order Copies of Dallas Cowboys Wives *The Dallas Cowboys Family "Playbook"*

to place your order on VISA or MasterCard:

PHONE: 1-800-678-8014, Ext. 101

FAX: 1-214-630-4098

MAIL: Trophy Publishing, 1200 Conveyor,
Dallas, Texas 75039 USA

Please enclose $16.95 per book, plus $4.95 postage/handling for the first book.
Add an extra $1 p/h for each additional book ordered.

Please send _____Cookbook(s) to:

Name ______________________________

Address ______________________________

City, State, Zip ______________________________

Credit Card Number ______________________________

❑ MasterCard ❑ VISA Exp. Date ______________________________

Signature ______________________________

Total Amount Enclosed ______________________________

Please make checks & money order payable to: Trophy Publishing.